111 95

Race Under Sail

Race Under Sail

Peter Hambly

STANFORD MARITIME · LONDON

Stanford Maritime Limited
Member Company of the George Philip Group
12 Long Acre London WC2E 9LP

First published in Great Britain 1978
Copyright © Peter Hambly 1978

Set in 11/12 Monophoto Imprint and
Printed in Great Britain by
BAS Printers Limited, Over Wallop, Hampshire
Jacket colour processing by
Technical Colour Laboratories, London

ISBN 0 540 07173 0

British Library Cataloguing in Publication Data
Hambly, Peter
    Race under sail.
    1. Tall Ships Race
    I. Title
    797.1′4   GV832
    ISBN 0-540-07173-0

The author and editor wish to acknowledge and thank
the following photographers and sources of
illustrations used in this book.

Giles and Lady Chichester, 16, 18, 21, 39, 75
Lipton Tea (U.K. Division) Ltd, back cover, 8, 15,
17, 60 top, 63 right
Roger Bonnett, front cover, 27 left, 46, 80, 82, 84
bottom, 87 right, 88, 94 middle, 97 bottom, 98 top,
100, 101, 110
Cruising World, courtesy Murray Davis, 29, 45
bottom, 47 bottom left, 50, 89, 90, 91, 94 bottom
Jonathan Eastland, 11, 37 left, 52, 58, 59, 60 bottom,
65

The Sunday Times, 18; Belgian Embassy, London,
30; Columbian Navy, 33, left; Royal Danish
Embassy, London, 12, 25 left, 33 right; E. C. P.
Armées (France), 37 right; German Embassy,
London, 40; The Agent General of Nova Scotia for
the U.K. and Europe, 31 right; Royal Swedish
Embassy, London, 51; Ocean Youth Club, 35;
Philadelphia Maritime Museum, 28 top; Sail
Training Association, 34; Maj. Chris Barne, 38, 108;
Maj. M. Richards and Crew of *Kukri*, 79, 105 top; Lt
Cdr Celestino da Silva, 76; Esmond Friend, 103; Cdr
H. M. Juta, 13, 68, 72, 95 top left; Tadeur Karwacki,
86 left; Zygmunt Kowalski, 67; Albert Siedl, 31 left;
Jack Spratt, 93 right; Barclay Warburton III, 26

Foreword

When Peter Hambly asked me to write a foreword to *Race Under Sail*, I was delighted. This book is a magnificent production with very good photographs and a lot of information about the race. *Gipsy Moth V* was sailed by Peter and crewed with three other men and three girls.

This yacht is very personal to me: it was my husband's last boat and he had planned to take me to the Pacific in her; we had started to discuss her layout in Portugal in 1969 and Francis drew out a plan on the patio of our villa.

Later we went to Ireland where she was built and I named and launched her; then I did the sailing trials with him. We sailed down to the Mediterranean to make a film, but I never got my cruise in her. My husband decided he wanted to face one more challenge on his own. The Mediterranean was too small for what he had in mind, 200 miles a day over 20 days. He did not quite achieve his ambition, but set up a record which has not been beaten so far.

Peter Hambly describes the exhilaration of sailing up the Hudson River in the company of other great ships. I had done this twice with my husband in *Gipsy Moth III*. The first time was in 1960. I went out to meet him off Ambrose Light Vessel in a press boat when he won the First Solo Race and then again two years later after his record breaking solo transatlantic passage. The second occasion I will never forget, for it was Independence Day and I had a telegram from President Kennedy in my pocket.

I know how happy Francis would be to see these young people sailing in *Gipsy Moth V* under this competent skipper, who brought her back in a perfect condition.

1978   *Sheila Chichester*

Acknowledgements

For Jen

I would like to thank: Lady Chichester and Giles Chichester for trusting me with *Gipsy Moth V*; Alan Thorne for his help; Julian Hill and everyone at Lipton Tea (U.K. Division) Ltd. for making the venture possible and for their support; Roger Bonnett from Stanford Maritime for knowing precisely when I needed encouragement with the manuscript and for his patient liaison with my editor Phoebe Mason. I'm grateful to John Hamilton, S.T.A. Race Director, for his enthusiasm and the useful information he gave me; to Roger Delves-Broughton, Minke Beetsma, Caroline and Rosemary Ferguson, Clive Bird and Roger Bonnett with whom I sailed *Gipsy Moth*; special thanks to Dave Mills who was the mate on board. The lady who typed is acknowledged elsewhere.

Contents

Introduction

An advantage of the modern welfare state is that we need no longer be primarily concerned with providing our daily bread. Should the individual suffer financial disaster, provision from the state for basic needs gives security against hunger. An enormous psychological restraint to guard against hardship has virtually been removed, and by choice we can pursue less basic needs. A new spectrum of activities has appeared which was not available to our parents.

My occupation for the past nine years has been sail training with an organization which specializes in taking young people to sea on cruises lasting anything from a weekend to four weeks. The normal range of the Ocean Youth Club's activities is anywhere that the time limit will allow, but seldom further afield than Stockholm or Corunna. Not so long ago, tired of the same areas, I organized a cruise with Swansea University Expeditionary Society to the West Indies. The voyage out and our visit to the islands was uneventful, but we returned to England across the North Atlantic in February.

Sailing conditions were bad, sometimes verging on appalling. The passage was not one that I would repeat for pleasure, but it was a turning point when I learned to treasure my life and to value the people around me. Everyone on board, whether they were cooking, steering or whatever, became an essential part of the team which drove the boat and as such were regarded for their personal capability, not by some grand yardstick remote from our situation.

There were occasions when people felt the need to seek higher authority for comfort. The fortunate may have achieved this through spiritual communication – an enviable security which I, while welcoming intercession from any deity, found impossible. My trick was to diminish the uncomfortable reality with an extravagant dream or idea. This was, at an embryonic stage, how *Gipsy Moth V* came to race with the 'Tall Ships'.

But why enter the Tall Ships Race rather than do anything else? The motives were mainly selfish. My preference is for long passages, and the 1976 series of races between England and America provided a chance to indulge this. Underlying it was a feeling based on the transatlantic experience, that a small yacht sailing on a long voyage and an enclosed environment provide a unique opportunity for something otherwise unobtainable.

In Britain, as in many other countries, sail training is now recreational rather than for the purpose of training professional seamen on sailing ships. Financially independent of the government, our system must rely on income from cruise fees, private donations and local educational grants. Money has geared the normal sail training range to one or two week cruises to such an extent that the established organizations seldom look beyond this. As charitable institutions they must be seen by their benefactors to be providing a tangible service: what other way is there of doing this than by showing in the annual report the maximum number of young people sailing for the minimum expenditure? Benefit to the customer, the thing that sail training should provide, is a nebulous commodity, not an enumerable statistic, and cannot appear on a balance sheet. 'Benefit' is altogether a difficult thing to explain. The gauge I use, although there must be better ones, is to decide at the end of a cruise whether or not a person could better have used their time on the Costa del Sol. It is a gauge without malice. Anyone who spends two weeks in abject misery on a boat could have used their money more appropriately elsewhere. However, in general the longer people are at sea (within tolerable limits) the more they appear to derive satisfaction from it. Combined with my own bias towards long cruises, this determined that we would have one crew for the entire voyage, which was to be in four separate races with the added attraction

provided by America's Bicentennial celebrations. From Plymouth, England across the Atlantic to America and back again to Plymouth.

The first leg, the Plymouth to Santa Cruz de Tenerife race, a distance of 1,424 miles, began on May 2, 1976. The initial fleet was joined by more competitors in Tenerife for the 2,517 mile race to Bermuda. There a large contingent of ships and yachts further increased the racing fleet to a total of ninety-six vessels for the short 627 mile hop to Newport, Rhode Island. The final race from Boston, Massachusetts back to Plymouth has a relatively informal affair intended to take the European boats back to Europe for August under competitive conditions. Of the four months for the whole series, around two-thirds of this time was spent at sea.

The Sail Training Association Races

The Sail Training Association (S.T.A.) was formed in 1955 in England to organize a race for the remaining square-rigged sail training ships of the world in the following year. That race was a success, and it was decided to keep the association to administer similar races every two years. These biennial events are known as Tall Ships Races, a name which may give the impression that all the vessels entered are square-rigged ships. This is not so; in fact the majority of the entries are fore-and-aft rigged and range from large schooners such as Sweden's *Gladan* to thoroughbred and comparatively tiny ocean racers such as *Carillion of Wight*. The basic requirements for entry in a Tall Ships Race are simple. A vessel must be thirty feet on the waterline and comply in its safety equipment with S.T.A. requirements. At least half the crew must be trainees or non-professionals between sixteen and twenty-five.

For racing purposes the craft are divided into two groups: Class A for the prima donna square-riggers of more than 150 tons Thames measurement. Other

Cadets on Danmark

vessels of 500 tons TM and over, and not square-rigged, are included at the discretion of the Committee. There is no upper size limit. Class B comprises all other sailing vessels over 30 ft (9.14 m) in waterline length, with any rig. Entries in Class B are generally subdivided into Divisions depending on the number of vessels taking part in a given event and in accordance with their size and sailing potential. Thames measurement is calculated

$$TM = \frac{(L-B) \times B \times \frac{1}{2}B}{94}$$

where L = length at deck level from fore side of stem to after side of sternpost; B = extreme breadth (beam)

excluding protrusions: in feet and tenths.

For the 1976 series of races the division of Class B was: Class B Division I, vessels racing without spinnakers; Class B Division II, vessels racing with spinnakers. Division within the fleet has enabled the S.T.A. to devise a handicapping system based on Thames measurement, rig and sail area which allows boats of differing types to compete on reasonably equal terms within their class. Handicapping cannot, however, compensate entirely for overall sailing conditions. Square-rigged vessels will usually outrun modern small yachts in heavy downwind going, while modern yachts invariably gain in light windward conditions. This at least was the accepted view until the recent races when the Russian ships *Tovarishch* and *Kruzenshtern* soundly thrashed all comers in light airs – a remarkable feat which won applause from some and their being dubbed *'Motovarishch'* and *'Dieselshtern'* by others. Russians apart, the only improvement to the existing handicap system that I can think of is to rate a vessel according to its S.T.A. track record, thereby lowering the Time Correction Factor (T.C.F.) for vessels frequently last and increasing it for consistent winners. Although a similar system is used in determining Portsmouth Yardstick ratings for more conventional boats, a suggestion of this sort would produce hysteria in ordinary ocean racing circles, where a boat is designed to win and the more often the better. In S.T.A. events winning is not necessarily the criterion. All sorts of other objectives are bandied about ranging from 'fostering international understanding' to 'the spirit of sail training'. I have never understood the latter, but an interpretation I enjoy is Baden-Powell reading Conrad.

A feature of the races which has been included since 1972 is the crew interchange and cruise in company.

The machinery which administers these races is remarkable. To bring ninety-six vessels together, sixteen of them square-rigged, and representing twenty-six countries is no mean achievement. Colonel Dick Scholfield, the S.T.A. Race Director, was the man responsible. Initial planning began four years ahead, although we only saw the completed package neatly wrapped up in a broadsheet called 'Provisional Arrangements'. A humble title for a comprehensive document which provided for contingencies ranging from what lights were to be shown by a vessel finishing at night in Tenerife to shower facilities available at Boston.

Dick Scholfield is a yachtsman of the old school. Formerly a part-owner of the ex Bristol pilot cutter *Theodora*, he began racing in the days when yachts hove to in strong winds. He was, I think, the first British skipper to continue racing to windward in gale conditions. He joined the S.T.A. in 1963 after his retirement from the Royal Artillery, and brought with him not only the qualities of his former profession but the flexibility and patience essential to those who sail seriously.

The sea is said to be a great equalizer of men, which explains perhaps why money seems to be a taboo subject in S.T.A. events. But without it the races couldn't happen, so I think it's worth mentioning that Cutty Sark Scotch Whisky have sponsored the Tall Ships Races since 1972. There are sponsors and sponsors – some insist on banners and gauche publicity, but in Cutty Sark the S.T.A. found ideal people who tempered publicity with prudence and obviously enjoyed being part of the races. It was always good to see John Rudd, Chairman of Cutty Sark, and his wife take the time from their official obligations to talk to the crews.

Masters are asked to nominate a given number of their crew to sail on other vessels; the organizers then perform a juggle with sums, nationalities and ships which resolves ideally in an amicable international melting-pot afloat. It is a particularly useful exercise for the big ships where formal routine makes impromptu social arrangements difficult. Smaller yachts seldom have problems getting together on a multi-national basis. For them the advantage of the crew interchange is the opportunity it provides to sail on large vessels. It sounds like an idealist's tea party, and generally it is. But to see the thing in perspective, there was the Cockney whom I, envious of his experience, asked what he thought of sailing on a barque. 'Bleedin' rotten,' he said, 'lousy food, properganda films, and we wasn't allowed to touch a fing.'

Finding a Boat

I have been fascinated by Metre-rated yachts ever since Britain challenged for the America's Cup with *Sceptre*. I remember quite clearly stealing my school's copy of the *London Illustrated News* which gave the preamble to the challenge. The idea to take part in the Tall Ships Race naturally came to be centred around *Sceptre*, which I knew to be lying unconverted in a shed at Lymington. My estimate for purchase, conversion and entering the race was approximately £35,000 and totally beyond my means. Commercial interest, considering the international nature of the event, was a possibility.

I contacted Allen Thorne, who had enthused over an earlier venture. Allen is Vice-Commodore of the Midland Bank Sailing Club and the manager of their Pall Mall branch. He was keen on the idea but doubtful that the bank would be tempted in a period of economic uncertainty. Allen's doubts were correct, and there followed a time when I approached various other companies with equal lack of success. The *Sceptre* dream was obviously too expensive, so I tailored my idea to the economy.

A St Ives mackerel driver was next in line. Built in the late nineteenth century, she had recently been renovated by Geoffrey Williams, winner of the 1968 Singlehanded Transatlantic Race, at the Ocean Youth Club yard near Falmouth. *Barnabas*, as she was called, had all the nostalgia of oakum and tar, which, failing the pedigree of a Twelve Metre, attracted me. She had the added interest of an unusual rig with a dipping lug on the mainmast and standing lug on the mizzen. Additional power could be achieved with a reaching staysail and a large jib set on a reefing (retractable) bowsprit. This would have been an ideal sail combination for trade wind passages, but with a ton and a half of internal shifting ballast not the best boat for tacking at close quarters. Perhaps providentially, *Barnabas*' owners, the Maritime Trust, decided that it was not within the Trust's charter to allow a vessel of theirs to sail outside British waters.

After the *Barnabas* disappointment I bandied various other thoughts about unsuccessfully. Then Allen Thorne, always true to his interest in the project, introduction to Giles Chichester, a customer at his branch, with a view to chartering the yacht myself. The Chichester family had never chartered *Gipsy Moth V* before and only considered doing so for the purpose of what would be a benevolent event. At our meeting Giles was cautious, with natural concern for the yacht, and it was apparent that he and his mother, Lady Chichester, regarded the yacht as an irreplaceable heritage. My own feeling for *Gipsy Moth* was not so intimate. I thought of her at that time as something of a national monument, a

The first of Sir Thomas Lipton's Shamrocks, *with which he challenged for the America's Cup.*

Sir Thomas Lipton

suggested the possibility of Midland Bank entering *Gipsy Moth V*. Would I skipper? There was no hesitation about that: I would.

Maybe my bank account firmly entrenched with Lloyds in a forgotten Wiltshire village had something to do with Midland and I never quite getting together. Their people, despite careful budgeting of the proposition, eventually decided against *Gipsy Moth V*. She was not to be given up so easily: I had sailed *Sir Thomas Lipton*, the yacht on which Robert Clarke had based her design, and if *Lipton* was anything to go by, *Gipsy Moth V* would be a flyer.

I asked Allen Thorne whether he would arrange an

feeling later to be endorsed with affection. Lady Chichester and Giles checked my credentials with care before they finally agreed. At last, the perfect boat was within reach. A major task remained – the elusive money for the running costs and charter fee.

Geoffrey Williams had written three thousand letters before he found sponsors for *Sir Thomas Lipton* to enter the Singlehanded Transatlantic Race, an admirable tenacity which indirectly led to Lipton Tea (U.K. Division) Ltd sponsoring *Gipsy Moth V*. In 1969 Geoffrey loaned *Sir Thomas Lipton* to the Ocean Youth Club as the spearhead of an operation to raise money for nine purpose-built ketches for the club. *Lipton* became a charge of mine, and in the winter of that year I worked in conjunction with Julian Hill (then Export Manager of Liptons) to organize a cruise to the Caribbean.

In my search for financial backing I had overlooked the natural sequence of contacting Liptons. When I eventually phoned, I discovered that Julian had become the Marketing Director. He invited me to an initial meeting, and at lunch a week later Julian and I discussed the whole project with Alf Boxer, Lipton's Publicity Manager.

Lipton Tea Company had recently come under the Lever Brothers umbrella and moved to new premises at Leighton Buzzard, Bedfordshire. Julian felt that the company's own entry in an event such as the Tall Ships Race could have a unifying influence on the staff, and would help to launch the new packaging on their teas which depicted sailing ships as a theme. Somewhere between the pudding and the coffee the idea came alive. Underlying Julian's commercial abilities there is a man who knows the value of dreams: such men understand difficulties but pursue their way while the less imaginative linger in uncertainties.

Sir Thomas Lipton
(facing page)

Gipsy Moth V *with
her race crew, at
Plymouth before the
start.*

Sir Francis Chichester's *Gipsy Moths*

Gipsy Moth V was the third racing yacht especially designed and built for Sir Francis Chichester. Originally described as the boat which he intended sailing round the world with his wife Sheila, in leisurely fashion, she was nevertheless a singlehanded racer.

After his circumnavigation in 1968–9, he felt that the ultimate test for the singlehander was speed. In *Gipsy Moth IV* he had competed against the time taken by the wool clippers from Australia via Cape Horn to the London markets, but had not achieved what he considered the blue ribbon of singlehanded sailing – 200 miles a day over a sustained period and between accurately established positions. A notable feature of many claims for clipper ships' twenty-four hour runs was the absence of reliable positions on the days before and after.

Chichester decided to race *Gipsy Moth V* along a great circle route, from Bissau in the then Portuguese West Africa to San Juan del Norte in Nicaragua, four thousand miles away, starting in January 1971. This route gave a distance, with fixed points of departure, of 200 miles a day for twenty days. Unfortunately, to get the full distance it was necessary to start fifty miles up the estuary of the Geba River in almost windless conditions, which meant only eighty-four miles made good in the first twenty-four hours. He picked up speed thereafter, and despite both running booms breaking and having to make a third from the remains lashed together, he sailed the 4000 miles in $22\frac{1}{3}$ days; a remarkable achievement, establishing a record for singlehanded sailing at speed which was accounted a 'failure' because he had not achieved his own target of 200 miles a day. The theoretical hull (near maximum) speed of *Gipsy Moth* is 8.7 knots, and Sir Francis maintained an average of 7.5 knots for $22\frac{1}{3}$ days.

In 1972 he prepared *Gipsy Moth V* to sail in the Singlehanded Transatlantic Race. He hoped this voyage would bring an improvement to his health, but getting on for halfway across, the effects of pain-killing drugs and prolonged illness made him decide it would be prudent to turn back, so *Gipsy Moth V* returned safely to Plymouth with her skipper for the last time. Sir Francis died less than two months later.

Gipsy Moth V was designed by Robert Clark, who had designed *Gipsy Moth III* and *Sir Thomas Lipton*. The hull has many features in common with *Lipton*, although *Gipsy Moth V* has a different sail plan as she was intended for fast sailing off the wind. Robert Clark devised a rig which he felt could be easily handled by one man: a staysail ketch based on three sails of heavy-duty Terylene (Dacron) which could be left permanently on booms while at sea. The 57 ft hull, built for maximum strength and minimum weight, is a triple-layered diagonal cold-moulded shell with laminated wooden frames, stringers, keelson and stem plus steel frames for added strength near the masts, which are aluminium and stepped on the keelson. The keel is a $7\frac{1}{2}$ ton iron fin bolted to the keelson; the displacement 17 tons. Apart from the addition of two temporary bunks constructed in the after compartment to accommodate the seven crew members for the Tall Ships Races, *Gipsy Moth V* is unchanged in rig and internal layout.

Where *Gipsy Moth V* was Sir Francis' ideal yacht, *Gipsy Moth IV*, in which he circumnavigated the world, was not. On his pre-departure trials in the Solent she heeled to 20° in a minor squall. The thought of such behaviour, magnified by enormous seas in the Southern Ocean, was a daunting proposition. It is a measure of Chichester that he even pursued his plans: that he should consider a race against the average time of 100 days taken by the wool clippers is amazing.

A speed target was, I think, a self-imposed discipline for Sir Francis; it enhanced his enjoyment in good times and made demands in difficult ones. His race against time was a personal affair beyond the need for external competition. Experience of ordinary ocean racing had passed with *Gipsy Moth II*. He must therefore have been surprised to receive a communication from Alec Rose, who wished to make a race of the circumnavigation using a derivation of Royal Ocean Racing Club rating by which *Lively Lady* would start several weeks ahead of *Gipsy Moth*. The suggestion, coming at a time when Chichester's intentions were not commonly disclosed, is puzzling. However, the contest never happened. *Lively Lady* collided with a steamer in the English Channel, and later fell on her side while drying out at Mashford's yard for repairs resulting from the collision. *Lively Lady* and *Gipsy Moth* might have seemed an unlikely match, but there were remarkable similarities in rig between the two yachts. Illingworth & Primrose, the architects of *Gipsy Moth IV*, were also responsible for designing a new rig for *Lively Lady*.

Sir Francis' circumnavigation captured the public's imagination. To me, following his progress from the safety of an armchair, it seemed an improbable adventure, and as each day of the voyage passed I expected the next to bring news of disaster. *Gipsy Moth*'s return to Plymouth brought thousands to watch from the Hoe and spectator craft. The British are not easily moved by notable feats, but with Chichester it was different. Children had plotted his reported positions on wall charts, old age pensioners felt younger, and our national introductory topic of conversation, the weather, made way for *Gipsy Moth* and her crew. It was an astonishing achievement which changed the whole spectrum of sailing. Where would-be world sailors had hesitated, their dreams now seemed possible. Events such as the *Sunday Times* 'Golden Globe' round the world singlehanded race and the similar subsequent races for crewed yachts became feasible. Someone may

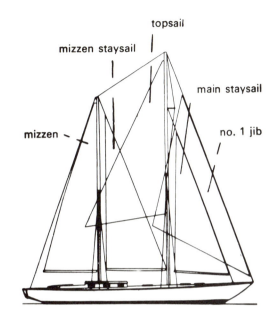

yet circle the world with one hand tied behind their back, but it was Chichester who began a tradition.

In 1976 the Singlehanded Transatlantic Race attracted over a hundred entries with yachts ranging in overall length from twenty to over two hundred feet. In the first race, conceived by Col. 'Blondie' Hasler in 1960, the 40 ft *Gipsy Moth III* had been largest of four entries and considered by some too much for one man to handle, especially someone who had never been alone in a boat bigger than a 12 ft dinghy. Age and his recent recovery from lung cancer were additional fuel for the sceptics. *Gipsy Moth III* won in 40½ days having sailed 4,004 miles to make good 3,000 miles on the great circle route.

Two years later Chichester again set off from Plymouth to cross the Atlantic alone. *Gipsy Moth III*'s rig, now altered from sloop to cutter, was easier to handle; the mast and boom were shortened, and to compensate for the subsequent loss in mainsail area larger jibs were made. With these modifications Chichester hoped to maintain an average speed of 6½ knots over a 30 day crossing. He arrived at New York on July 4, 1962, three days after his target date but

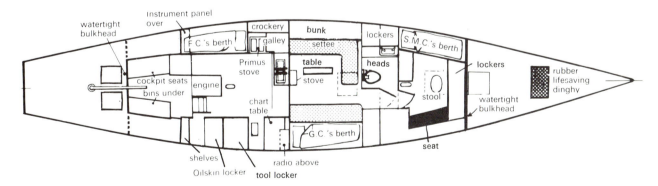

Sailplan and layout of
Gipsy Moth V.

coincidentally the day on which, fourteen years later, *Gipsy Moth V* joined the Bicentennial Parade of Sail along the Hudson River. This crossing held the singlehanded record until 1964 when Eric Tabarly sailing *Pen Duick II* won the Singlehanded Transatlantic Race; *Gipsy Moth III* came second. The winning boat had been designed for the race, and at the time it was felt that this was an extreme and not quite sporting measure.

Long before Sir Francis took to sailing he was known for his adventures as an aviator and navigator. Of all his flying exploits, which included a singlehanded flight from England to Australia, the first solo crossing of the Tasman Sea in 1931 brought him recognition as a pilot extraordinary – especially among fellow aviators, who were intrigued by Chichester's navigational adeptness and innovation. Navigation became a passion with Chichester; in fact one of his reasons for buying his first yacht *Gipsy Moth II* (named after the aircraft) was as a means to continue practical navigation.

Gipsy Moth seems a gentle name for the tool of so many adventurous exploits.

The Ships and Their Crews

Radio communications were a feature of the race series. Each vessel was obliged to carry a medium wave transmitter/receiver for daily position reports to the communications vessel, which in its turn passed the information back to the S.T.A. race headquarters. John Hamilton was the Assistant Race Director at the time (he has since Col. Scholfield's retirement become the boss) and had overall responsibility for coordinating schedules. He also ensured that dissidents like myself werc obliged to carry a wireless, pushing the safety angle and a view that radio would 'add another dimension to the race'. My feeling was that it would destroy the solitude which I value at sea. On balance I think John was right. Wireless chats became the highlight of our days and provided interest and information which outweighed my nebulous insularity.

The great thing about the radio was that we got to know other ships and fancied that from the operators' tone we could gauge the mood and progress of our competitors. Sailing vessels at sea tend to have a day-to-day mood. When the going is good the crew follow suit, but let the ship sit becalmed for a day or two and the sullen atmosphere born from helplessness permeates the ship and gradually underminds her people.

Through radio we came to know the fleet. We associated a voice with a ship, and the voice seldom belied the man or woman behind it. This, then, is a small picture of the ships and crews who sailed them. It is perhaps more informative about the vessels that sailed all the way from Plymouth than those which joined the fleet at Bermuda. We had little time to meet the people who came solely for the third race. Nor could we, with only five days at sea for that event, get to know them by radio.

A full list of all the vessels which raced is given in the Appendix; the following section is meant to indicate the variety of national approaches to sail training, and a selection of the many different kinds of boats which sailed in the S.T.A. Race.

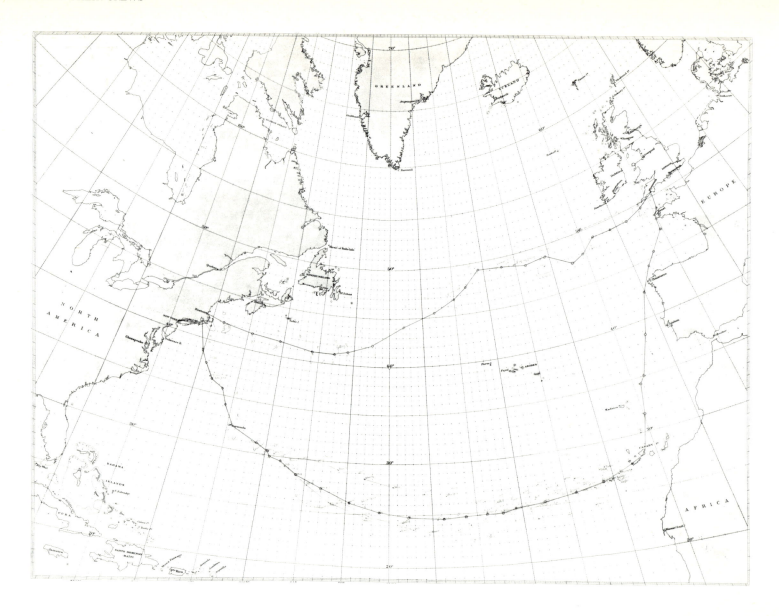

The tracks of Gipsy Moth V *and a few of her close competitors over the four stages of the Tall Ships Race (facing page).*

Cadets working in Denmark's *rigging (left), and U.S. Coast Guard cadets on* Eagle.

America

The United States does not have vessels specifically built for recreational sail training comparable to Britain's fleet of ketches belonging to the Ocean Youth Club, or to the two S.T.A. schooners. Privately owned yachts or vessels affiliated to private educational establishments provide the usual means of training under sail in America. The U.S. Coast Guard barque *Eagle* is an exception, but the experience she provides is available only to male officer cadets of that service. It is surprising that with its maritime tradition and wealth America has produced only one vessel, *Brilliant*, to compare partially with the British and European sail training blueprint. A further limitation on deep-water sail training *per se* is a U.S. Coast Guard regulation which restricts many large vessels to cruising within twenty miles offshore, unless they fulfil exorbitant requirements for crews and equipment. Fortunately, oceanographic or marine biological research programmes exempt sailing vessels to a degree and allow them to continue operating.

Since 1964 American vessels have twice appeared at sail training functions. In 1972 *Eagle* and *Black Pearl*, a hermaphrodite brig owned by Barclay Warburton III, President of the American Sail Training Association (A.S.T.A.), joined a race from England to the Baltic. Two years later the schooner *America*, a replica of the famous winner of the America's Cup, raced from Copenhagen to Gdynia in Poland with a Danish crew.

In 1976 the only yacht registered in the U.S.A. to race back from Tenerife was the yawl *Saracen* sailing with Bermudan trainees. None made the full series, though a number joined the fleet at Bermuda for the last leg.

It was a member of *Saracen*'s crew who, in a television interview, did much to illustrate the diversity of conditions aboard sailing vessels. He referred to the hardships of the Atlantic crossing in terms of water rationing which, on *Saracen*, meant that showers were only allowed twice weekly. On other yachts even more economy was necessary, and the crew of *Gipsy Moth* can't be the only ones obliged to brush their teeth with salt water.

For people who know little about sailing it is reasonable to assume that sailors arriving in port on a yacht or sailing ship do so having experienced similar comfort or discomfort. This is not so: I would, for instance, feel uncomfortable under the formal discipline essential to a big-ship routine, whereas a big-ship sailor might find a yacht claustrophobic. Seasonal considerations also came into this, as on *Polonez* which did not have a fixed marine toilet. Morning rituals were performed to the shout 'Nie patrzyé' (No sightseeing!) from the stern pulpit – a tiresome arrangement in December but perfectly adequate for the summer.

Twenty-nine American vessels joined the fleet in Bermuda for the race to Newport, Rhode Island. The Sea Education Association at Woods Hole, Massachussetts entered their schooner *Westward* with a female crew to compete for the Cutty Sark Trophy awarded for the first vessel with an all-girl crew to finish on handicap. Other contestants for this trophy were *Sir Winston Churchill* (United Kingdom) and *Astral* (Netherlands Antilles). *Westward* and *Astral* retired from the race because of their slow progress in light airs,

giving *Churchill* the trophy by default.

Many of the United States vessels are normally used for educational purposes related to oceanographic and marine biological research. By contrast, *Unicorn* forms part of a rehabilitation programme which specializes in male youths who have appeared in Florida's courts on charges of drug abuse, breaking and entering, and theft. The Associated Marine Institutes which run the scheme estimate that their eighty per cent success ratio in this field is higher than the national average.

Unicorn is a superb 140 ft wooden brig originally built as a schooner by the Finnish government after World War II. She was one of thirty-three similar vessels specifically designed to carry timber and sand, essential materials for the rebuilding of Finland's war-damaged towns. Later *Unicorn* was used purely as a motorized sand barge. A reprieve from this pursuit came when

The privately owned brig Black Pearl *(facing page), the research vessel* Westward *(above), and* Unicorn *(right).*

Jacques Thiry acquired and re-rigged her using the sail plans of the 1876 French brig *Adolph & Laura*. She now has modern fittings and electronic gear below, and a 500 h.p. diesel engine.

The late William Wychoff Smith provided the money for *Unicorn*'s refit. His generosity also enabled the Philadelphia Maritime Museum to buy *Gazela Primeiro*, the last of the Portuguese Grand Banks schooners. In her fishing days *Gazela Primeiro* was the mother ship for thirty-one dories, each worked by a fisherman with half a mile of line with 600 baited hooks. The men rowed off from the mother ship at dawn, cast their lines throughout the day and returned at dusk. By this means it was possible, though unusual, for each dory to land a thousand pound catch.

Gazela Primeiro was built in 1883 and has hardly altered since she last fished on the Grand Banks in 1969. Her copper-sheathed bottom has protected the hull, planked with maritime pine. A 'dining out' feature which the owners have retained is the shower, which consists of a nozzle attached to the bottom of a water keg mounted on the side of the galley. It is filled by buckets from the galley pump.

At the other end of the American entries were the charter boats. Most famous of them was the pre-war (1936) Francis Herreshoff designed *Ticonderoga*. She is an ocean racing legend in America, holding at one time just about every race record there was on the western side of the Atlantic. The Time Correction Factor she was given in Bermuda for these races shows that Herreshoff's genius is less appreciated in England. On rating, *Gipsy Moth* was obliged to give time to *Ticonderoga*, an 87 ft ketch. That the latter finished twenty-seven hours ahead shows how much the American yacht's performance was underestimated.

Gazela Primeiro *(above) on her departure from Philadelphia for the third leg of the race, and before she lost her topmasts at the start off Bermuda.* Eagle *(below) was unscathed and able to race to Newport.*

The U.S. Naval Academy was represented by four 48 ft fibreglass yawls, *Active*, *Dandy*, *Flirt* and *Fearless*. They finished the race at Newport in that order and within four hours of each other, thus taking third to seventh places in their division. They further showed their paces with a spectacular display of spinnaker sailing during the New York Parade of Sail.

America's pride, the U.S. Coast Guard barque *Eagle*, has had her traditional Blohm & Voss lines transformed by the red Coast Guard emblem painted on her white bow section from bulwark to waterline. The emblem was a controversial idea which led the appropriate authorities to seek opinion poll guidance: regardless of a contrary vote, they then got out their paint pots. Perhaps the adage 'Not only do, be seen to be doing' determined the Coast Guard's decision to pursue their colour scheme.

Libertad at Newport

Antigua, W. I.

The Antiguan schooner *Freelance*, built of iron in 1907 on the Clyde, nearly sank thirty miles south of Bermuda on passage for the race. The crew took some time to find an inaccessible leak by the stern gland, and preparations had already been made to abandon ship when it was discovered. *Freelance*'s skipper radioed for help, which was given by a passing freighter. Bermuda Radio, hearing the distress call, arranged for two large pumps to be sent out to assist with bailing out. The schooner was saved and started in the race as scheduled. *Freelance* later retired, but I am uncertain whether it was for lack of wind or as a continuation of her earlier problems. Judging by the number of engineers and amount of engineering equipment strewn on the yacht's decks in Newport, it may have been the latter.

Argentina

It occurs to me that the scarcity of sailing ships has resulted in the moderately interested person never having the opportunity to develop an eye for their aesthetic design. Anything with a square sail is generally admired. An example of such debatable praise is *Libertad*. Two authoritative sources to my knowledge refer to her in the following terms: 'Visitors crowded aboard in wonder at her size and beauty', and more conservatively, 'The ship has an imposing appearance.' Perhaps the second 'authority' quietly shuddered at the modern bridge set between the fore and main masts and a deckhouse with a chimney further aft. These structures ruin the appearance of an otherwise pleasing ship. That *Libertad* is clearly conceived for training young men into a mechanized Argentine Navy probably justifies the clumsy additions. Twin Sulzer engines aligned to a single shaft give engineer midshipmen the means to learn their skills. Would-be deck officers are

Zenobe Gramme, *in which a tall rig was coupled with powerful diesels.*

able to practice their art from a bridge similar to those they may expect to work on in the future.

Belgium

Prior to the race, the Belgian Navy had toyed with a thought to replace *Zenobe Gramme*'s two powerful engines with a single light diesel to improve the sailing performance of the 95 ft wooden ketch. Time and a tight schedule providentially decided them against the idea. It was those engines which led Lt. Georges Saille, her Captain, to be awarded the Cutty Sark Trophy, given biannually to the vessel which has, by majority vote of the fleet, done most to 'foster international understanding'.

Zenobe Gramme had towed two yachts, *Erika* (Switzerland) and *Kukri* (U.K.) a thousand miles through the calms on passage to Bermuda.

Canada

The barquentine *Barba Negra* joined the fleet at the eleventh hour in Bermuda. Originally built in 1896 in Norway, she is now normally involved in marine research, although she did take part in the 1974 Tall Ships Race from Corunna to Southsea. I saw her early in the following year at anchor in English Harbour, Antigua, flying a skull and crossbones pennant at the masthead.

During the race from Bermuda to Newport the owner's children followed *Barba Negra*'s progress from a motorboat. In the calms they were taken on board and asked to stay with their father. Because the children were under the minimum age allowed by the rules, he subsequently retired from the race.

Four other Canadian boats, *Pathfinder*, *Playfair*, *St Lawrence* and *Bluenose II* took part in the Parade of Sail.

Barba Negra *(left)*

Bluenose II *(right)*
*was built in the same
Lunenberg, Nova
Scotia yard, and by
many of the same men,
as the original Grand
Banks fishing schooner.
Her famous predecessor
was launched in 1921
as a saltbanker and
became the undefeated
holder of the
International
Fishermen's Trophy,
raced for by American
and Canadian working
schooners. Although she
survived longer than
her rivals, Bluenose's
loss on a Haitian reef
in 1942 was the
occasion of national
sorrow.*

Of these, *Bluenose II*, an exact replica of the famous Nova Scotian fishing schooner, built in 1921 at Lunenberg to capture the International Fishermen's Trophy raced for by American and Canadian working schooners, was especially interesting. The story goes that the original *Bluenose* deviated slightly from the lines drawn by her designer William Roué, and that this led to her success in racing. The yard certainly built up the fore sections to give more headroom in the forepeak, but whether the hull lines were altered remains in dispute. It was not unusual at the time for builders to loft every third or fourth frame leaving those in between to the shipwright's eye, and this might have contributed to *Bluenose*'s exceptional performance. Later schooners were unable to repeat her success.

Chile

The Chilean navy's four-masted barquentine *Esmeralda* is virtually the same as Spain's *Juan Sebastian de Elcano*. Both vessels were built at the Cadiz yard of Echevarrieta y Larrina, and designed by the British yacht designers and builders Camper & Nicholson. The second of the pair, *Esmeralda* was laid down in 1942 as an additional vessel for Spain, but fire damaged the partially built hull and delayed completion until 1951, when she was launched under a Chilean government contract.

At Newport the U.S. Coast Guard patrolled a security area a hundred yards wide around *Esmeralda* to keep possible demonstrators at bay, following allegations that the vessel was used as a torture ship for political prisoners after the 1973 coup in Chile. The captain and crew were embarrassed by the restriction on sight-seeing craft, but the Coast Guard stuck to their instructions. In view of events at New York where

Esmeralda at sea with everything set.

demonstrators threw bottles of red paint over *Esmeralda*'s decks from the quay, it was probably a good thing they did. It is sad, though, that politics should mar a vessel that came with goodwill.

Arc Gloria (left), and the pre-war training ship Danmark (right), built after the unexplained loss of the five-masted barque København in the winter of 1928–9, with all sixty hands, including forty cadets.

Columbia

The barque *Gloria*, built in Bilbao for the Columbian Navy in 1968, was developed from the pre-war Blohm & Voss lines used for *Eagle*, *Gorch Fock II* and *Tovarishch*. In common with *Eagle* she began life with a divided spanker but has since changed to a single sail. At 249 ft overall, *Gloria* is shorter than her predecessors. Her lines are impaired by a large bridge and wheelhouse at the forward end of the poop, and by another deckhouse built from between the main and mizzen masts to the forecastle.

Denmark

The ship-rigged *Danmark* is well known in America. She was in Florida when the Germans occupied Denmark in 1940, and after Pearl Harbor was handed over to the U.S. Coast Guard for cadet training. Captain Knud Hansen retained command throughout the war and afterwards sailed his vessel home. Hansen's wartime effort had instilled the training under sail concept with the Coast Guard, however, and his suggestion to requisition the German barque *Horst Wessel* was enthusiastically pursued; she was brought to America and re-named *Eagle*.

In the race, *Danmark* terrified her Bermudan pilot when she sailed through the narrow entrance of St George's Harbour, Bermuda under full canvas except for courses (the huge lowest squaresails on each mast) and docked hardly using her engine.

Sir Winston
Churchill, *owned and
run by the Sail
Training Association;
and the Ocean Youth
Club's* Master Builder
(facing page).

England

The British yachts (other than *Wandering Star* and *Valeda* which joined at Bermuda) sailed the complete circuit incorporating two Atlantic crossings. With the exception of *Gipsy Moth*, all changed crews at the beginning of each leg. *Sir Winston Churchill* visited St John's in Newfoundland after the Boston Parade of Sail and subsequently did not join the race home to Plymouth. Until the fleet reached Bermuda the British were second only to the Poles in their variety of vessels, ranging from the S.T.A.'s 153 ft three-masted topsail schooner *Sir Winston Churchill* to *Carillion of Wight* a Sparkman & Stephens designed 47 ft sloop, sister yacht to Mr Heath's ill-fated *Morning Cloud*.

The Ocean Youth Club's 72 ft ketch *Master Builder* represented an organization which has in recent years become the largest sailing scheme in England, and yet for its size remains the least known. The O.Y.C., founded in 1960, sailed with mixed crews at a time when ladies on boats were considered an affliction. Its objectives, even from its formative years, were to use the sea as a medium for social education as opposed to the 'heave and pull for the benefit of your character' attitude prevalent at the time in most organizations. It is interesting that the S.T.A., comparatively new to the recreational sail training field, is tending towards a similar outlook. Lord Burnham, their Vice Chairman, Sailing, wrote in his article for the official race programme, 'The "third dimension" of education which until recent years has been somewhat neglected is the art of living together in mutual harmony and cooperation and voluntarily accepting a necessary discipline for the achievement of a common object.' Both organizations rely heavily on cruise fees to pay their way, so no matter what their philosophy, ultimately they must keep the customers satisfied.

Different money criteria apply to the London Sailing Project, which is subsidized by Viscount Amory's Rona Trust. The Trust runs its vessels on naval lines with emphasis on the training of crews through progressively longer cruises. For the Tall Ships Race the London Sailing Project (L.S.P.) chartered *Great Britain II*, the 85 ft ketch built for Britain's sailing entrepreneur Chay Blyth and his crew of paratroopers to compete in the 1973–4 Whitbread Round the World Race, and since used for other similar events. Woolworths provided the charter fee and the crew were asked to make a substantial but reasonable contribution towards the running costs. The nature of the organization enabled the L.S.P. to select their crews by the same procedure used to select officers for the Services, although the qualities they required were not necessarily the same; for instance, 'need to go' in emotionally or otherwise deprived cases was given special consideration. Rumour had it that another factor was the ability to sing the first verse of 'Rule Britannia'. Anyone who knew the second hit the jackpot.

Outlaw and *Carillion of Wight* are normally based at Cowes. Robert Fewtrell, owner and skipper of *Outlaw*, sailed on *Moyana* as a trainee in the first Tall Ships Race in 1956. Nostalgia from that event gave him the determination to buy his own yacht for 1976. To Robert's chagrin and our amusement, never during the four months we heard him did he manage to say 'Outlaw' over the radio-telephone without adopting an Anglicized Australian accent. I think 'Carillion' could be a derivation of the word 'carillon' (an air played on bells), which seems an appropriate name for a yacht belonging to the Christian Sailing Centre.

The British Army entered *Kukri* and *Sabre*,

Kukri and Sabre *tied up with fellow competitors at Tenerife.*

Nicholson 55s similar in hull design to *Adventure* which had come second on handicap in the original Whitbread Round the World Race. A yawl rig gave *Sabre* some advantage over her sister ship in reaching conditions, but with winds from any other quarter, and especially in light airs, *Kukri*'s sloop rig paid off.

Cameo of Looe and *Charm III* are privately owned. *Charm III*'s withdrawal from the entire series after only two days' sailing was a great disappointment to those on board. A skipper who enters a vessel for a Tall Ships Race has a special responsibility to fulfil his contract to the crew. They have after all arranged their time and brought their dreams and expectations to sail. Uncertainty of purpose and inadequate preparation, whether emotional or of the boat, seem out of place to me.

Bel Espoir II *(left)*
and the French Navy's
goelette Belle Poule
(right).

France

Centre Nautiques des Glénans is a unique, no-nonsense sailing school based primarily on the Isles Glénans, a picturesque archipelago a few miles off the south Brittany coast, having the only coral beaches in Europe. The Centre has subsidiary bases in Southern Ireland, the Mediterranean and in other parts of France. Government subsidies enable the organization to cover a wide sphere of teaching in sailing craft ranging from dinghies to ocean racers. Pupils joining the Centre start at the bottom of the ladder and must work through the curriculum regardless of their previous experience – a system which gives France the nucleus for a national sailing standard.

Young men and women who passed through this Centre Nautiques a decade ago are now in the financial position to own their own yachts, and at sea they are among the finest yachtsmen in Europe. It is only in harbour that an omission in the Centre's training becomes noticeable. The protégées of the system have had little, if any, tuition in using auxiliary engines. I can't be the only one in a crowded anchorage who thinks of the small print on the insurance policy when a Frenchman starts his engine.

Glénan, a 47 ft cutter similar in design to *Outlaw*, represented the Centre Nautiques des Glénans. She was brilliantly sailed, particularly during the first and last legs.

Although she was unable to take part, *Bel Poule* attended the start at Plymouth. She is one of two Paimpol *goélettes* built in 1932 for the Ecole Navale, and has been in many sail training races. Such vessels sailed regularly between Newfoundland and the north coast of France in the nineteenth century.

Bel Espoir II, a topsail schooner built in Denmark in 1944, is sailed by the Amis Jeudi Dimanche, and arrived at Plymouth with a crew largely too young to meet the S.T.A. age rule. She was not allowed to race as part of the fleet, but followed the same route across to the U.S.A. and back.

Germany

International understanding is a byword in the sail-training vocabulary. My experience of this 'understanding', admittedly gained from small boats, is that opportunities for informal get-togethers happen more frequently among the yachts than with the large training ships. Beyond the enjoyable spectacle of a big square-rigged ship, it is difficult to identify with the crew who

Germania VI, sighted from Kukri *on the last race of the series.*

sail her. Among the small boats, we knew the people on board and wished them well or otherwise.

Stortebeker, a 53 ft club boat from the Hamburgischer Verein Seefahrt, became a special friend to *Gipsy Moth*. The club was formed at the beginning of this century by the Hamburg City Guilds to give ordinary people the means to participate in a sport dominated at the time by British crews. In those days, owners brought their yachts to Cowes to compete in annual regattas, and regardless of nationality employed British sailors, usually fishermen who became professional hands in the summer, to race their vessels. The Hamburgischer Verein Seefahrt provided the money to enlist, for the first time, an all-German crew.

Where *Stortebeker* obviously thrived on canned beer, *Germania VI*, an 80 ft yawl which once belonged to the German industrialist Krupp, enjoyed champagne. The Arndt von Bohlen und Halbach-Stiftung, her present owners, are fairly exclusive and not easily drawn to conversation.

The Federal German Navy's barque *Gorch Fock II*, launched in 1958, is the last of a line in training ships

Gorch Fock II, the German naval training ship (and preceding page).

built by the Blohm & Voss yard at Hamburg. She has sailed in more S.T.A. races than any other Class A vessel and is, in race results, the most successful. Her captain from 1964–8, Hans Engel, had organized the German contribution to Operation Sail held at Kiel during the 1972 Olympics and now skippered *Carola*, a beautifully renovated 83 ft Baltic galeas or trading ketch (built in oak in Nykoping, Denmark in 1900) in the final Boston to Plymouth race.

Berlin's Academischer Segler-Verein never achieved the potential one would expect from *Walross III*, a 56 ft Bermudan sloop designed in 1971 by Sparkman & Stephens. On the fourth leg her skipper, Claus Reichardt, a medical student, heard disturbing noises from the keel. Suspecting the worst, keel delamination, he reduced canvas to nurse his vessel home to Europe. In a calm seven days out from Boston, Claus sent an inspection party over the side to discover that *Walross* had dragged a small mooring buoy for some 1200 miles.

Radio communications are a problem with a fleet where ships' speeds vary, and we were grateful to the ketch *Tina IV* which assisted, and never failed to demonstrate the power of her medium wave transmitter.

Grand Cayman Islands, B.W.I.

Two converted 125 ft Baltic trading schooners, usually based in Denmark, use the Cayman Islands as a flag of convenience. Dieter Kluckow, the skipper and part owner of *Gefion*, sailed on the ill-fated *Pamir* three months before she sank in 1956. He reckons to have ridden through five hurricanes in twenty years at sea. Kluckow and his partner now pursue a less hazardous occupation: they buy, refurbish and sell Baltic traders, and also organize charter trips from Copenhagen, taking guests for two or three week cruises. *Gefion* was built in oak in Solvesborg, Sweden in 1894.

Gefion *in the Canary Islands, with* Sagres *at anchor in the background.*

Brian Watson spent two years restoring *Lindø*, a three-masted topsail schooner built in Sweden in 1929, for charter work. Lucrative guests sailed with him until Boston where the sail training idea seemed to catch on. He loaded *Lindø* with trainees for a fee which barely covered their food. Considering that normal charter guests were invited to pay between five and six hundred pounds for three weeks, it was a fairly philanthropic move.

Ireland

Erskine Childers is best remembered outside Ireland for his classic adventure sailing novel *Riddle of the Sands*, first published before World War I. Within Ireland, the man and his yacht *Asgard*, which he once used for running a consignment of arms, have found a place in the country's history. The Irish government bought Asgard in 1964 as a national monument and for simultaneous use in sail training, a situation which led her skipper to comment, 'We've the only sailing monument afloat.' By 1975 *Asgard* was too old to continue the training programme and she was replaced, as an interim measure, by the 49 ft Bermudan ketch *Creidne*, which sailed in the S.T.A. Race.

Another vessel registered in Ireland, although normally kept in Holland, was the 102 ft *Phoenix*. Chartered by Mariners International (which was involved with *Second Life* in the first Whitbread Round the World Race), *Phoenix*' claim to fame was the chickens kept in a specially constructed weatherproof coop on deck. To supplement the crew's egg diet and provide historic authenticity, traditional dried peas, beans and lentils were also carried on board.

At 151 tons TM *Phoenix* was the smallest Class A vessel. Her three-masted barquentine rig, reminiscent of Baltic traders in their heyday between 1880 and 1890, proved inefficient compared to the fore-and-aft rigged Baltic traders (ketches and schooners). By a quirk of the rules, *Phoenix* was because of her squaresails unable to sail in the same class with them.

Italy

The Italian yawl *Stella Polare* and *Germania VI* have similar hulls, but unfortunately the two yachts never

Amerigo Vespucci *(above) and* Urania *(right).*

Netherlands

The Royal Netherlands Navy's Bermudan ketch *Urania* was a ship that appeared to find the happy balance between informality and naval discipline. She was built in steel in 1928, and the gear on board was of the heavy traditional variety, which irritated her crew in light airs when a sail change from genoa to spinnaker could take as long as thirty minutes. Heavy gear also gave problems in stronger winds – *Urania*'s largest spinnaker, admittedly an ancient creation, fell apart irreparably during a minor puff. Her skipper, Fritz Reedeker, either resourceful or in fury, tore the

raced against each other. *Stella Polare* sailed races two and three and *Germania* races one and four. Franco Faggioni, *Stella Polare*'s skipper, is an enthusiastic racing yachtsman who competed in the 1972 Single handed Transatlantic Race. In his professional capacity as a Captain in the Italian Navy he once commanded *Amerigo Vespucci*, a training ship built on the lines of a nineteenth century frigate.

Amerigo Vespucci is usually an honorary guest at sail training functions. Being heavily constructed and under-canvassed compared to other training vessels, though ship-rigged, she is not competitive; in light winds she must rely on her engines to maintain sailing schedules. *Amerigo Vespucci* took part in the New York Parade of Sail.

remnants into suitable lengths and distributed necker-chief souvenirs among the fleet.

The Dutch Sail Training Association's schooner *Eendracht* is organized on much the same lines as the Ocean Youth Club vessels during the summer, although the fees are much higher and make her cruises available only to the reasonably well-off. In winter the schooner is used for Mediterranean charter work in an endeavour to subsidize the normal sail training programme, a scheme which according to reports in the Dutch press has achieved some success. Further revenue for the S.T.A. Race was raised by a public relations firm, which then charged a higher fee than the amount raised. *Eendracht* is beautifully fitted out below to accommodate her charter guests, giving trainees incomparable luxury at times when she is being used for her designed purpose.

Watersports Twellegeo entered their 61 ft ketch *Norseman*, sister ship to their *Dutchman* and *Irishman*, for the complete series, with crew changes at the beginning of each leg. Vessels belonging to the organization normally visit ports anywhere north of Ushant. It is one of those fascinating sailing schemes which do things (they previously entered *The Great Escape* in the *Financial Times* Clipper Race to Australia and back) and yet it is difficult to discover anything about them. I understand that their yachts are run on a similar basis to the O.Y.C. but without an upper age limit. Cruise fees on *Norseman* are roughly the same as on *Eendracht*.

The 84 ft pre-war gaff ketch *Jacomina* was wrecked on the North African coast on passage to join the S.T.A. fleet at Tenerife. Her crew was rescued, but the vessel became a total loss.

Eendracht

Netherlands Antilles

A condition for participating in the New York Parade of Sail was that a yacht or ship should sail in at least one S.T.A. or A.S.T.A. race of the series. Therefore it seemed to me a natural conclusion that the crew on board for the race should remain with the vessel for the parade, a point which escaped *Astral*, among others. *Astral*'s owner supplemented his permanent staff with a trainee crew of girls, thus making his yacht eligible for the Cutty Sark Trophy awarded to the first all-girl crew to finish on handicap. In the calms on the third race, *Astral* retired, but nevertheless it was a great opportunity for the girls. It is a pity that the owner did not extend his generosity beyond Newport, where some of the crew were deposed in favour of the owner's friends who were taken on board for the Parade of Sail.

Norway

Christian Radich is to me the prettiest ship in the S.T.A. fleet. Slightly smaller than most of the Blohm & Voss training ships, she has better proportions than the larger vessels built to pass under bridges along the Kiel Canal.

Whereas most cadets have signed on the dotted line to become merchant or naval seamen before they join ship, on *Christian Radich* cadets finally decide whether to become professional sailors after they have served on board. This seems a typically considerate Scandinavian system to decide one's career, which, if the enjoyment her crew derived from the experience was indicative of the final result, appeared to be a good method.

Christian Radich's cadets joined the ship only a few days before departure from Norway. Light westerly winds meant that the passage to Plymouth was mostly under engine, giving little opportunity to gain sail handling experience. The permanent crew had a bit of a

Astral

Christian Radich

job on their hands at the Plymouth start, but by Tenerife it was a different story. Young men, some barely fifteen, exuding bravado, bowled along the streets of Santa Cruz with the gait of veteran Cape Horners. To see the development of *Christian Radich*'s crew between England and America was interesting: they began everything as uncertain children, and became confident young men.

On the return passage from America *Christian Radich* hove to during a severe storm in the western approaches to the English Channel. Her sails and rigging were damaged but she was able to fetch Falmouth for temporary repairs.

Mexico
Ramon Carlin bought *Sayula II*, a standard ketch-rigged Swan 65 design, for the 1973 Whitbread Round the World Race. In that event his successful approach was to look after the 'inner man'. The cocktail hour was rumoured to have been rigidly observed, with drinks served on a silver platter as a prelude to a four-course dinner. Quite the opposite idea to Chay Blyth's regime, where his crew on *Great Britain II* lived on dehydrated foods which they ate with spoons. (Knives and forks, considered unnecessary weight, were not carried on board.)

The race between Bermuda and Newport was easy going and too short to make crew psychology a decisive factor. *Sayula* improved on her 1973 success by beating *G.B. II* over the line as well as on corrected time.

Panama
Three vessels, *Te Vega, Candide* and *Erawan*, raced under the Panamanian flag from Bermuda to Newport. *Te Vega*, a 156 ft steel schooner built in 1932 in Kiel and

Te Vega

Poland

Geographical position has made Poland the historic buffer state for territorial maurauders. Occupation by Germans and Russians has given the Poles a unique national pride, expressed in the quality of their produce, the hospitality of the people, and in recent years, the quality of her sportsmen, who exude their enjoyment.

Of all the national entries, Poland's yachts probably required most organization. The country has foreign currency problems and consequently her yachts must keep expenditure abroad to a minimum. Thus they stocked up with and carried their major victuals for the entire voyage – a considerable handicap in weight, which goes some way to explain their improved performance during the Bermuda to Newport race by which time a large part of these stores had been used. Further economies were made possible by the practical ability of the crews, who coped with any gear failure ranging from minor sail repairs to comparatively difficult engineering work to hull and rig fittings. It was a pleasure to observe the Poles' self-reliance. Their independence of fancy modern chandlers was a great example to anyone who wants to sail economically.

now owned by the Flint School in Florida, normally sails worldwide on educational cruises sponsored by the Education and Research Corporation of Sarasota, Florida. She is in effect a floating classroom for junior and senior high school pupils, both boys and girls.

The regular sail training fleet was joined at Bermuda by a number of vessels normally employed for charter work. *Erawan*, an under-canvassed 150 ft wooden barquentine from the Caribbean, was one of these. She and the other Panamanian vessels retired from the race during a spell of light winds.

A friend of mine had planned to join her at Boston for a cruise to Montreal, but fortunately decided against the idea. *Erawan* sank on the return passage from Canada.

Dar Pomorza was the flagship of the Polish entries. A full-rigged ship built in steel in 1909 for the German School Ship Association, she was handed over to France at the end of World War I as part of the reparations. The French government had no use for her and sold *Colbert*, as she was called at the time, to a private owner who planned to convert her as his yacht. This proved a pipe-dream, and she was sold again in 1927 to Poland which has used her ever since to train merchant officers.

Her Captain, K. Jurkiewicz, joined *Dar Pomorza* as a cadet in 1931. He was on board when she sailed for Stockholm at the outbreak of World War II. The ship

Dar Pormoza, *and Kris Baranowski in the cockpit of* Polonez.

Zawisza Czarny *at Newport, and* Polonez *anchored off Sandy Hook with the famous American yacht* Ticonderoga *in the background.*

remained under the protection of Sweden's neutrality for the duration of the war, to resume service unscathed afterwards. Meanwhile Jurkiewicz, by then a watch officer, led a group of her people back to enlist in the Polish Army. His courage during the war and his physical strength are legendary. He is reputed to have carried *Dar Pomorza*'s kedge anchor, weighing 800 lbs, on his back along the length of the main deck.

Cadets on *Dar Pomorza* are not permitted to wear safety harnesses aloft at sea, which in the safety-conscious seventies is an indication of the aura that surrounds her captain. The Polish authorities do not hinder his view that harnesses are prissy and un-necessary.

Dar Pomorza won the first Sail Training Race she took part in, and afterwards joined the Operation Sail Fleet at the Kiel Olympics in 1972. She raced again in 1974 with the S.T.A. fleet from Copenhagen to Gdynia.

Another national hero in the Polish team was Krzysztof Baranowski (Chris) sailing *Polonez*, the 50 ft ketch in which he competed in the 1972 Singlehanded Transatlantic Race, followed soon afterwards by a singlehanded circumnavigation. *Polonez* turned turtle on three separate occasions during her world cruise, and when I first met Chris as a fellow competitor in the 1972 S.T.A. Southsea to Cherbourg race he was still clearing up the disorder from a knockdown off the Needles. Despite the mess, he won the race but was disqualified on a technicality which requires at least half the crew to be trainees under twenty-five years old – an in-surmountable problem for someone over twenty-five sailing alone.

The rapport between the crews of *Gipsy Moth* and *Polonez* began with polite nods, progressed through occasional cups of coffee with Baranowski's deceptive cherry vodka, until Tenerife and afterwards when we became honorary musicians for the *Polonez* band. Our talent lay in Roger Delves-Broughton who can play anything from a mandoline to a trombone. Roger's recitals were refreshing interludes in a spontaneous noise produced by us lesser musicians on anything that would bang or clang. *Polonez* taught us the odd pleasantries in Polish, and something else for which I remain grateful: the correct pronunciation of '*Woje-woda Koszalinski*'. Only someone who has suffered the depreciating glance of a Frenchman directed at a foreigner attempting his language, as I have, can understand the joy of rattling off a tongue-twister.

When *Gedania* from the Gdansk Shipyard Yacht Club joined the fleet at Bermuda, we were interested in her used appearance. Paintwork was worn and rust streaked, sails patched, and her rigging seemed too old for that side of the Atlantic. Later we heard that *Gedania* had come by the difficult route – from Poland, an attempt at the Canadian Northwest Passage, then South through the Panama Canal to the Antarctic; finally north again by way of Cape Horn to the West Indies and Bermuda.

Portugal

The shipyard of Blohm & Voss produced three virtually identical barques between 1933 and 1938 for the German Navy. All three continue in their role as training ships although they are now registered under different flags.

The first, launched in 1933 as *Gorch Fock I*, is now *Tovarishch*. *Horst Wessel*, the second off the stocks, is now *Eagle*, and lastly *Albert Leo Schlageter,* launched in 1938, was renamed *Sagres II* in 1961 having spent the interim years on the American and Brazilian register.

Sagres *coming into Newport Harbour (left).*

Juan Sebastian de Elcano *setting topsails prior to the start at Tenerife (right).*

Red Portuguese crosses on her squaresails easily distinguish *Sagres* from the other Blohm & Voss barques.

Her Captain, Fernando Gomes, is the most courteous man I have ever met. He conducts his life with impeccable grace and with humour. At Newport, some friends and I were invited to *Sagres* for a final drink after a dance. We sat in the Captain's day cabin, a fairly imposing room, when the door flew open to reveal a bedraggled young man, presumably a guest on board. 'Hey, you guys, where do you keep the John on this tub?' he asked. Fernando gave him directions along the corridor to the third door on the left. Seconds later, the same untidy figure reappeared: 'Where did ya say the . . . ing thing was?' Fernando stood up and politely escorted him to the loo.

Spain

Tenerife won her division for the Plymouth to Santa Cruz de Tenerife race, but she was not the *Tenerife* which the crew originally planned to sail. Two weeks before the start, while being prepared for shipping to England, her cradle broke. The yacht smashed down onto the freighter into which she was being loaded, bounced off, and sank. Undeterred, the crew sent for divers to salvage removable equipment, packed their bags and flew to London to buy a new boat. They found a 34 ft sloop within three days, stored up and soon afterwards raced her home.

Spain's giant four-masted barquentine *Juan Sebastian de Elcano* boasts a chapel. The naval officers and men on board sing the *oracion* at seven every evening, thereby observing a centuries old tradition:

Tu que dispones de viento y mar
Haces la calma, la tempestad
Ten de nostros Sẽnor piedad
Piedad, Sẽnor; Sẽnor piedad.

Roughly translated, 'You who command the wind and sea, make calm into a storm, have mercy Lord.' Magellan's sailors used this prayer on their arduous and eventful voyage of 1519. In five boats, 240 men set off from Spain; a year later they cleared the Straits into the Pacific, which Magellan named 'Mar Pacifico' (peaceful sea). In 1521 he was killed by natives in the Philippines and Sebastian de Elcano took command. He and sixteen other Europeans finally returned to Spain after the first circumnavigation. It had taken three years.

The routine on *Juan Sebastian de Elcano* is run on strictly naval lines with deference to Catholicism. Almost four hundred people on board function to train sixty-three of their number as future officers. Cadets are selected third year students from Spain's Naval Academy.

Sweden

The Royal Swedish Navy operate the two-masted gaff schooners *Gladan* and *Falken*. The former vessel sailed the entire circuit from Plymouth to Plymouth with, had there been an overall placing, outright success. To see a 133 ft steel schooner handled like a dinghy is a rare experience. *Gipsy Moth V* sailed within sight of *Gladan* on two occasions and we were amazed by her performance. Helmsman and crew responded to the slightest wind shift, heavy sails were hoisted or lowered with the apparent ease of an Admiral's Cup boat racing in the Solent. Even when she was out of sight, we followed *Gladan*'s progress with keen interest from the daily

Mircea II, and the figurehead of the prince after whom she is named.

position reports. She was after all in our division, and on handicap our nearest rival.

Perhaps the incident which finally won my total admiration for *Gladan* happened during the calms a few hundred miles short of Bermuda. There was a tentative move, encouraged by the communications vessel *Sir Winston Churchill*, a schooner comparable to *Gladan*, to cancel or finish the race at sea. *Gladan* would have none of it and carried on. Flexibility and imaginative tactics enabled her to wriggle round the calm while the less adaptable continued to bewail their misfortune.

For the final transatlantic leg, Boston to Plymouth, *Gladan* took on the job of communications ship. Whereas in the first two races vessels had guarded their weather information, *Gladan*, equipped with receivers that could pick up forecasts from either side of the Atlantic, re-transmitted the reports for everyone's benefit. She supplied a nice touch which lifted the event above the cut and thrust of ordinary racing.

Switzerland

Built in 1900 for Denmark's Icelandic fishing industry, *Ericka* was constructed with heavy scantlings to cope with Arctic conditions. Her wooden hull, now painted bright yellow, needs a gale or a powerful engine to shift it.

We came to regard *Ericka*'s late arrival at terminal ports with affection. Unfortunately, as a result of these prolonged passages we seldom had the opportunity to meet her crew, who barely had time, after arrival celebrations, to pack their bags and catch the plane.

Ericka was bought in 1970 by a group of Swiss enthusiasts who spent four years renovating the ketch to her original condition. The Cruising Club of Switzerland entered her in all four races with crew changes between each one.

Rumania

The barque *Mircea II* was built by Blohm & Voss for the Rumanian government's Merchant Marine Nautical College and on completion sailed immediately for a base at Constanta. Launched in 1938, *Mircea* postdated her sister ship *Albert Leo Schlageter*, now *Sagres II*, by some months. Of all the training ships from the

The Swedish naval schooner Gladan.

same yard, these two are most evenly matched.

Mircea takes her name from the Rumanian prince who by force of arms won back the Dobrugea region from Turkey in the fourteenth century. Restoration of this coastline enabled Rumania to establish herself as a sea power.

Russia assumed control over *Mircea* after the war, but she was soon returned to her owners and resumed service with the merchant marine.

Russia

Padua, as *Kruzenshtern* was called before the Russians requisitioned her after the war, was built in 1927 in Bremerhaven for the Hamburg shipowner F. Laeisz to join his famous Flying P Line. She was the ultimate development in bulk carriers, a 378 ft four-masted barque designed to be handled by a crew of thirty seamen. Even then, provision was made in her accommodation for forty cadets. It was in a vessel similar to *Padua* that the famous German captain Hilgandorf doubled the Horn for ten consecutive years working in the Chilean nitrate trade, at an average speed of $7\frac{1}{2}$ knots. Hilgandorf, admittedly a legend in his time, was said to have padlocked his halliards to the mast in heavy weather. His performance does show, however, that given the right vessel, with the right man in charge, a credible sailing speed even by today's standards is possible.

Padua was renamed after the first Russian to circumnavigate the world, Admiral Adam Johann Ritter van Kruzenshtern. The Fishery Board of the U.S.S.R., *Kruzenshtern*'s present owners, recruits cadets from Russia's farmlands for induction into the fishing industry – labour deployment which led an uncharitable friend to comment, 'They're catching

Tovarishch *(facing page) and* Kruzenshtern.

whales with pitchforks.'

Tovarishch was originally *Gorch Fock I*, a 270 ft three-master built for the German Navy in 1933. She was sunk off Stralsund in 1945 and salvaged by the Russians in 1948.

The Russians first entered *Tovarishch* and *Kruzenshtern* in the 1974 Tall Ships Race from Copenhagen to Gdynia, Poland. I sailed in the same race and thought it uncanny that *Tovarishch* beat the Twelve Metre yacht *Evaine* in ideal Twelve conditions. Rumour had it that *Tovarishch* failed to round the northern course mark, giving her some forty miles advantage. We dismissed the whispers; it was inconceivable that anyone would cheat in a Tall Ships Race. *Kruzenshtern* was awarded the Cutty Sark Trophy and both boats were feted. *Entente cordiale* was the game to play. Everyone slapped each other on the back, congratulating themselves that the Soviet Union had joined the fleet.

Many competitors held the view that *Tovarishch* and *Kruzenshtern* motored during the calm spells in the Bicentennial races.

Preparations

Mashford's yard – *Gipsy Moth*'s winter home – is in a communications backwater on the Hamoaze at Cremyll, across the estuary from Plymouth. Cremyll is difficult to find by road, leaving the area delightfully unspoilt. Access is possible for foot-passengers by way of the Stonehouse ferry which plies the River Tamar, and although the ferry's existence is no secret it is not widely advertised, which further isolates Cremyll.

Late in March 1976 some friends and I made our way to Mashford's to prepare *Gipsy Moth* for sea. The yacht was to be launched on the day following our arrival, but from the ferry we saw her already lying to her mooring with masts stepped. *Gipsy Moth* has since become a familiar sight, but time has done nothing to diminish that initial joy at a yacht perfectly proportioned and yet so purposeful that the world's oceans seemed undaunting to her.

In the following days while we put stores and spares aboard, Sir Francis Chichester again won my admiration. Items which could go wrong had a spare neatly contained in one of many Tupperware boxes. The yacht worked: lockers were provided with convenient hinges; each hook or bolt had a purpose. The cockpit bins were filled with additional cordage, blocks and rigging. *Gipsy Moth*, bar catastrophe, was an independent entity equipped to sail anywhere.

Giles Chichester joined us to unravel what were to me the mysteries of her topsails and running sails, and to assure himself that his family heirloom was safe. We left Mashford's on a Friday evening's tide for Alderney in the Channel Islands. The wind died outside Plymouth breakwater, giving the opportunity we needed to practice sail changes in comfort. The starboard log impeller fouled periodically, making a nonsense of our dead reckoning position. Consequently an indifferent landfall on the following day came as no surprise. We spent a pleasant evening at supper with Biddy Worsley in her home on the island. Biddy's husband George was my colonel from Army days and he taught me more about sailing than anyone. He died in 1974, but

Gypsy Moth's *crew on the chilly passage to Plymouth : from left, Caroline and Rosemary Ferguson, Roger Delves-Broughton, Minke Beetsma and Clive Bird. Dave Mills, the mate, is below making coffee.*

planned to carry, obliging me to find the cash for a new one. Worst of all, *Gipsy Moth*'s feathering propeller refused to engage from the sailing position. This first happened in the approaches to the Hamble River after a day sail in the Solent. It happened again the following weekend when Julian Hill and Allen Thorne came to sail for a luncheon party at Giles' club in Cowes. Fortunately he had arranged to meet us at Cowes Roads with Lord Montagu's launch. We were towed alongside, but with a strong northeasterly wind the Groves & Gutteridge pontoons were untenable. Julian and Allen leapt ashore clutching their lunch suits while Clive, one of our race crew, and I set off for home.

Tacking a 57 ft boat up the Hamble is something which I would prefer to avoid, and I was pleased, hoping for a tow, to see an inshore rescue boat. Clive shouted across to their bosun, who looked back with that special scorn reserved for idiots who navigate the river under sail for pleasure. We secured *Gipsy Moth* to the moorings with nothing worse than a graze on her starboard topside. I remain grateful to the man (he never gave his name) who rowed out in bleak conditions to attach our line on the upwind pile.

All the problems seemed to resolve themselves when *Gipsy Moth*'s full racing crew arrived two days later. Dave Mills, whose judgement I trust implicitly (we sailed the Atlantic together in 1975), was the natural choice as mate. Not only was his navigation better than mine, he retained more interest in the subject than the little I ever had. His greatest contribution to the crew was to temper my inconsiderate periods with understanding and unobtrusive concern. It is hard to come by a better friend than that.

The second mate, Clive Bird, looked to have been born with salt water in his veins. Sensitive ladies from

Alderney remains the place from which I prefer to begin or end special cruises.

Later that night we weighed anchor bound for the Hamble River, my home base. After breakfast Giles explained the intricacies of the running rig, and we spent the day playing with the appropriate sails. By the time *Gipsy Moth* reached her temporary mooring at Hamble, Giles had shown enough confidence in the big running booms for me to overcome my fear of decapitation from that source.

The next two weeks were a nightmare of preparation and of sleepless nights spent planning for remote contingencies. Not only the inevitable little niggles were annoying. Delivery of the radio-telephone was delayed. The liferaft people condemned the raft which I had

Plymouth to Boston gazed wishfully beyond the beard at Christopher Columbus and The Old Man of the Sea reincarnated as one. They may have been right, but for practical purposes Clive had the strength of three ordinary men, a valuable asset on the foredeck and at the winches.

Caroline Ferguson once sailed with me in a snowstorm. When the mate and other members of the crew collapsed into their bunks that night, Caroline provided endless mugs of hot chocolate while I steered, and I did likewise during her tricks at the wheel. Our depression differed only in that she could smile at a sunless dawn and I could not. This admirable ability led Caroline and her younger sister Rosemary a year later to join the crew of *Gipsy Moth*. On long passages crew relationships invariably go through phases of difficulty. The Ferguson sisters have my lasting appreciation for their ability to adapt to these phases and somewhere along the way find time to smile.

Our medical needs, which seldom went beyond an aspirin, were administered by Minke Beetsma, a Dutch girl who had trained in the nursing profession. Minke's sailing experience amounted to a few days in a dinghy on the Ijsselmeer. Natural enthusiasm and practicality quickly overcame inexperience to make her the star female foredeck hand.

Entertainment, especially musical, was Roger Delves-Broughton's forte. Roger's way of life as one of five actors in a travelling company performing in South Wales gave him an astute understanding of the ridiculous. His humour excelled in Gallic parody. Afro hair and complicated guitar-accompanied harmonies earned him his nickname 'Garfunkel'.

Finally, the eighth member of our crew was Roger Bonnett, with whom I had enjoyed some of the best cruises from O.Y.C. days. Work commitments delayed his joining until Bermuda and for similar reasons he was obliged to leave at Boston. In his professional capacity as the production director of Stanford Maritime, Roger proposed this book. His administrative ability was a great help in organizing the *Gipsy Moth* project.

For ordinary ocean racing, choice of crew is simple. Suitably skilled enthusiasts are recruited or trained, and providing the yacht is up to it there is with luck a possibility of success. The solution is not so easy when the crew must race and live together for three to four months: compatibility then becomes a major concern. Deciding is a gamble. The obvious alternatives are to find people of similar backgrounds such as Chay Blyth's paratroopers, or to use the other extreme, people with diverse temperaments and interests. I am inclined towards the latter, which is generally less stultifying but carries greater risk. On *Gipsy Moth* we were lucky. Our honeymoon with the yacht and with our situation lasted beyond Bermuda. Thereafter vague aggravations were sensed from time to time, but these never matured and in retrospect seem trifling.

One notices, living in a confined space, the minutest characteristics of one's companions. Mannerisms can become a source of annoyance verging on paranoia. For example, I can remember the intense and totally irrational irritation I felt at the way someone in our crew checked on their waistline when emerging from the cabin into the cockpit. Such irrationality is a universal problem on a long cruise, and I have yet to meet a crew from any yacht who has not been affected by some measure of it. Common sense and underlying goodwill held *Gipsy Moth*'s crew together, even on the last leg home when yachts with specialists in formal discipline had difficulties. It was good for us to rest from each other's company back in England, but now we would happily repeat the cruise together.

The last few days of preparation on the Hamble were miserable, especially for Clive and Garfunkel whose job it was to repair the ratlines and service the rigging in near-freezing conditions. From conscientiously tightening marline Clive's fingers were badly cut, which briefly put his hands out of action. Minke and Dave dashed from chandlery to chandlery in pursuit of forgotten items, and in between their buying forays found time to sort the charts. As stores arrived, Rosemary made space to stow them. Caroline typed contents lists for the Tupperware boxes and having recently completed a fancy cookery course assisted with victualling. Powell Engineering unravelled the propeller nause, R.F.D. came up with the liferaft as promised, the radio was fitted, and we all went off for the weekend to say our goodbyes. On Monday, April 26 we slipped our moorings bound for a press reception at Beaulieu before cruising to Plymouth.

The trouble with press receptions is the display one feels obliged to make. The photographs and smiles bit went marvellously. Problems began when we sailed away. Reaching down-river in perfect conditions was superb, but the leg running parallel to the Solent was to windward, obliging us to short-tack. On the fourth tack the jib's leech caught on the crosstree ends. A similar mishap three weeks later would have been quickly sorted out, but as a result of our unfamiliarity with the boat reactions were slow and in the interval between snagging the sail and bringing it down on deck eight feet of seam tore apart. An inauspicious beginning which emphasized the need for efficient teamwork.

Gipsy Moth carried the west-going tide past Portland Bill, scudding along at nine knots under twin headsails,

Our first sight of Dar Pormoza.

balloon topsail and mizzen. Lyme Bay opened up and to port we saw our first square-rigged vessel motoring on a converging course. As the ship approached magic happened: staysails shot up their stays and were sheeted home. Seconds later, squaresails were set to the wind. The evolution from beginning to end had taken three and a half minutes. Under full canvas, the ship made an effortless ten knots as she overhauled us. When her counter came abeam we recognized the Polish flag. It could only be *Dar Pormoza*; to which we dipped our ensign. The salute was returned. *Gipsy Moth*'s name had evidently come within binocular range, judging from the number of people watching her progress. That we should meet *Dar Pormoza* before any other big ship was appropriate. She of all the Tall Ships became the one with which we shared a special bond. We were flattered in Tenerife when her First Officer referred to

Gipsy Moth as 'our little sister'.

As night crept over the English Channel *Dar Pormoza* disappeared into the dark. By midnight Start Point lighthouse flashed our landfall. The running sails were handed and we altered course for Plymouth. In the early morning *Gipsy Moth* lay to her familiar moorings at Mashford's. Later I made arrangements with Sid and Theo Mashford to dry her out against their grid. The starboard log impeller had fouled excessively from the beginning, which led me to suspect that the weed deflector had broken off. I was also keen to see how the special antifouling I had asked for was behaving. Theo suggested coming alongside on the early tide of the following day. This left time until then to reorganize stowage, particularly in the cockpit lockers where the sheets, guys and other assorted cordage were kept. Dave instigated a simple system for finding the right rope for the job which overcame the confusion we had experienced on passage to Plymouth. I was obsessed by the time it took to hoist running booms and sails, and set about imparting my recently acquired knowledge to everyone on board. Ultimately we devised a method where everyone became interchangeable. The person setting up the stem paraphernalia knew what was happening at the mast and at the cockpit winches, and was as capable of performing those jobs as his or her own. That at least was the ideal we worked towards: the necessary skills came a little later.

On the following day my suspicion about the weed deflector was confirmed. Mashford's phoned around nearby chandlers but were unable to find a replacement off the shelf. Undeterred, their blacksmith fashioned one in bronze and fitted it within the tide.

When *Gipsy Moth* refloated we made fast to the buoy and rowed ashore for a surreptitious peep at the

Rat-guard on Dar Pormoza.

Phoenix, Gefion *and* Lindø, *seen under the bow of* Dar Pormoza *(facing page)*.

opposition assembling in Millbay Dock.

There was something daunting about the Sail Training Association's Race Office during the opening phase of the race, especially for unshaven skippers wearing jeans. The S.T.A. hierarchy were there to welcome ships' masters. The Race Director, Col. Dick Schofield, had that inscrutable air which came from many similar meetings and endeared him to us all. John Hamilton, his assistant, beamed a welcome from across the room. An executive lady asked whether I had come to collect my race instructions: if so, I couldn't have them unless I submitted a crew list. John Hamilton, quick to recognize unease, stepped in with an ambassadorial explanation that many skippers seemed reluctant to part with their crew list and to inveigle one out of them had become a minor tactical exercise. Since I

Directors of Liptons hand over a large consignment of tea prior to the start, at Plymouth.

Reflections on Millbay Dock: the Dutch schooner Artemis *is tied up outside* Christian Radich.

hadn't brought mine, I understood the point.

At the western end of the Millbay Dock, *Phoenix'* crew rigged a block and tackle derrick to lower a new gas oven on board. In Millbay's southeastern corner *Great Britain II*'s shanty group, standing on deck under an enormous Woolworth's banner, gave a quick 'What shall we do with the drunken sailor?' and 'Rule Britannia' recital to a quayside audience. *Charm III* had stowage problems with a mountainous lager delivery. Further along the dock *Christian Radich*'s crew were painting their ship, attending to rigging and lowering boats to practice for the Tenerife rowing competition. An aura of unconcerned, but nevertheless purposeful, preparation exuded from the ships' people in general.

Of the boats in *Gipsy Moth's* class it was difficult to assess their comparative rated performance. Other than the O.Y.C.'s *Master Builder*, which was unlikely to be a threat, the other vessels were unknown competition. In our ignorance we were not dismayed by an obvious flyer, *Gladan*.

Early the following morning we took *Gipsy Moth* round to join the fleet in Millbay Dock. The crew from *Stortebeker* beckoned a welcome so we made fast alongside. Preparation was complete; it remained only to order duty-free drinks, fresh meat and vegetables. On the eve of the start my wife Jen and our children joined us. Shortly afterwards friends from Lipton Tea Co. came along for the pre-race celebrations. They brought out tea stock and 'infusions' with them.

Giles Chichester and Roger Bonnett came to join the party, but our fears and anticipations for the following day subdued easy expression of the enjoyment we felt. The conflict between excitement to leave and leaving those we cared for was everyone's private problem.

Race 1 – Plymouth to Tenerife

The square-rigged vessels were first away. *Kruzenshtern* made sail with dignity, and a well-timed start put her first across the line. *Dar Pormoza* followed, demonstrating her panache at sail handling by hoisting full canvas in three minutes forty seconds. (Knowing what to expect, Clive kept a stopwatch handy to time them.) The Norwegians on *Christian Radich* pulled halliards and braces with all the enthusiasm of their youth. Occasionally crew members bubbling with excitement peered over the rail to wave at spectators on passing pleasure craft; alert watch officers redirected the cadets' attention to their official duties. *Tovarishch* delayed at anchor and may have had problems weighing it; poor visibility made it impossible to tell from our position. *Phoenix* chose to start further towards the middle of the line than the other Class A ships. This lost her some windward advantage but avoided the main cluster of spectator craft gathered at the western end.

Class B Division I, our division, were next to start. *Gipsy Moth V* was first to cross the line which made the approaches we had practiced earlier worthwhile.

With a seventeen knot southwesterly *Gipsy Moth* exceeded expectations sailing to windward. It was gratifying to see her sail upwind and draw away from *Master Builder*, another yacht from Robert Clark's drawing board, which with a longer waterline length should theoretically have outpaced her. Further optimism for *Gipsy Moth*'s comparative speed came an hour or so later when the racing machines in Class B Division II caught up. Clive, stopwatch still dangling round his neck, found that although the 85 ft *Great Britain II* (scratch yacht in Class B Division II) was overtaking, she was not doing so quickly enough to succeed on handicap. A few other yachts from Division II were coming by to windward causing some concern on board, but we regarded their progress philosophically, taking heart from *Gipsy Moth*'s downwind reputation. After all, the Pilot Charts predicted ideal sailing conditions for her between Cape Finisterre and Tenerife.

The start of Race I: Class A ships set sail and pick up speed before crossing the line.

By late afternoon the fleet had spread across the Channel leaving only two sails vaguely visible on the horizon. The BBC's 6 p.m. weather report for shipping forecast a gale affecting our area imminently. (In BBC forecast jargon 'imminent' means within six hours.) Obviously there was no way to avoid the weather entirely, although I understand *Master Builder* tried unsuccessfully to do so by tacking west. My hope was

that we would round Ushant, thus enabling us to bear off before the full force of wind found *Gipsy Moth*. This hope was not to be. Soon after midnight, during Dave's watch and still some fifteen miles downwind of Ushant, it became necessary to replace the No. 1 jib with the No. 2 and hand the mizzen. An hour later even the No. 2 jib overcanvassed us. Dave and his watch handed the sail and secured it along the lifelines. This is a normal

The naval guard ship marking the end of the line stands out from the spectator fleet; ashore, the hills surrounding the bay off Plymouth were crowded with watchers.

practice in racing which I continue to use, but one which the conscientious cruising man regards with scorn, rightly so judging from our experience a few hours later. The sail was barely secured when Dave dashed through the waves and spray from the foredeck to the cockpit shouting 'Have you seen it?' 'Seen what?' I asked, feeling the adrenalin coming to standby. 'Fine on the starboard bow – lights.' There, hardly 400 yards away,

the navigation lights of a large steamer appeared through the murk. It was too late to gybe and *Gipsy Moth* could not come about under only fore and main staysails. I bore off and at the last moment put the helm down to hold *Gipsy Moth* in irons while the steamer passed. As the apparently endless hulk churned by I clearly remember thinking how stupid it was that all the labours of the past months should end so ignominiously:

run down by a steamer not even a day out from Plymouth. Then I looked up to see the ship's stern light appear above *Gipsy Moth*'s mizzen: we were clear. The numbed shock lasted a minute or two. I glanced at Dave who glanced back, and we both knew how lucky we were to be looking at each other.

Fifteen miles ahead, *Great Britain II* had similar problems. With her main down on deck for reefing, a steamer appeared on a collision course. The jib sheet parted, obliging the yacht's skipper to put her about. During this exercise the remaining sheet skiffled up making the jib useless canvas flogging in the gale. David Cobb (her skipper for the first leg) had no alternative but to motor clear. Shortly afterwards a second, potentially more dangerous, problem arose. *G.B. II* began to take water at an alarming rate. The influx was only stemmed when the pipe to the main bilge pump (driven by the engine) was led aft. Conditions became particularly bad when fumes from a leaking exhaust pipe filled the below decks space. At one stage the entire crew donned lifejackets and the liferafts were cleared to abandon ship. A search party traced the leak to the after compartment where food boxes stored for the second leg had fallen against a seacock, dislodging the hose. The crew sorted out the problem, shifting packing cases while waves broke over the deck. Cynics at Plymouth, myself included, had wondered how *G.B. II*'s comparatively inexperienced crew would cope with their huge thoroughbred machine. 'Enthusiasm' was the retort from the crew and their organizers. If enthusiasm was their meteor, it certainly appears to have carried them through their difficulties, although a better incentive than a sinking ship is difficult to imagine.

When night made way for a cold and humourless dawn, the foredeck became tenable again. Clive and I

went forward to hoist the jib and discovered that a securing had come adrift in the dark. The sail was badly torn from snagging against a split pin. We hoisted an alternative and brought the damaged sail below where the non *mal-de-mer* sufferers spent eight hours working in rotation stitching it together again.

At 9 a.m., well past Ushant, the first call of the pre-set radio schedule with *Sir Winston Churchill* began. Judging from the reported positions, *Gipsy Moth* was not the only boat to have reduced sail in the night. *Kukri* and *Sabre* came through unscathed, but otherwise the weather had affected the smaller yachts' progress. *Stortebeker* had sailed over her genoa while handing it; *Master Builder*'s sheets parted; *Artemis* put in to Falmouth with rudder damage, and *Charm III* retired permanently from the race with various defects.

After the radio schedule, I switched the engine on to recharge *Gipsy Moth*'s domestic batteries. It started perfectly, spluttered, then died. Finding the fault was simple but unpleasant in disturbed sea conditions. Salt water had found its way into the fuel tank. Clive wedged a plastic bucket under the fuel filter, disconnected the bowl, then as the boat heeled to 13° or more, water from the tank discharged into the bucket. Three gallons of

Gefion chases Lindø out of Plymouth.

performed a swanky sail change at extraordinary speed, intended to demoralize *Walross'* crew. Whether or not the desired effect was achieved, I don't know. The only tangible result I could see was that *Walross* followed suit and hoisted a larger jib. *Gipsy Moth* drew ahead less rapidly than when the whole business began.

During the remaining eight days at sea we made a further fifty-six sail changes of one sort or another. I mention it now so that the procedure need not appear in the text again. I have in mind the view of a close friend, whose opinion I value. He once said, 'It takes a good writer to maintain my interest through the third sail change and a genius beyond the fourth.' I make no claim to either category.

Life on board improved as *Gipsy Moth* approached Cape Finisterre. The wind gradually dropped and shifted from southwest towards the north. Steamers, heard but unseen in poor visibility, motored by. Seasickness, the malaise which reduced willing spirits to lethargy, gradually disappeared among our crew. We progressed from being strangers, drawn together apparently at random, to a tight and integral part of our charge. *Gipsy Moth* became our dictator. We responded to every demand she made, trimming, hoisting and lowering sail for the slightest advantage. In turn she performed magnificently, bowling along with all the confidence of her pedigree. When strong northeasterly winds set in off the Portuguese coast, boat and crew were in harmony, exuberant in the freedom of the breaking seas, exaltant with speed. *Gipsy Moth* tore along showing never less than ten knots on the speedo. Twice in wild surfing conditions the needle passed the maximum twenty knot mark.

Gladan, hareing along in similar weather but some one hundred miles behind *Gipsy Moth*, accidentally

water collected in this way before familiar pink diesel appeared. The trouble recurred regularly until Tenerife when Dave traced it to an obscure hole in the side of the filler cap opening socket. In his book *The Romantic Challenge* Sir Francis Chichester complained of water in the fuel tank, and who knows, it could have been attributable to the same source.

Somewhere in the fuel crisis we overhauled *Walross III*, passing within shouting distance. I asked them to report our predicament to *Sir Winston Churchill* on the next radio schedule. Retaining power in the batteries for *Gipsy Moth*'s wind and speed instruments seemed more important than giving our daily position, and I was grateful to *Walross* for sending our message the following day.

Coincidentally the sail repairs were completed as the two yachts passed. Garfunkel, Rosemary and Clive gybed. Her main boom swept across the deck to carry the topmast preventer and main runner away. The topmast, deprived of its backstays, bent forward, broke, then crashed down to leeward. With typical efficiency *Gladan*'s crew cleared away the carnage, set up a jury running backstay and resumed course in less than two hours. Losing the topmast deprived the schooner of the use of the sails normally associated with that mast and cost her first place. That she finished only forty-nine minutes after the eventual winner was by any standard some feat of seamanship.

Not only the loss of spars caused concern on the first leg. Trouble with the generator while crossing the Bay of Biscay decided *Phoenix*' retirement to Corunna. The defects were quickly repaired, which enabled her to rejoin the fleet at Tenerife.

Meanwhile *Gipsy Moth* came within thirty miles of Madeira. Our spirits, high with the speed we were achieving, soared, as the sun, with signs of permanence, broke through the clouds. The wind dropped to an undemanding level and our oilskins were discarded for the first time in eight days. Bikinis and bathing trunks, until then merely cherished hopes, suddenly became realistic. Our world was transformed in a few hours from exciting bedlam to recuperative lethargy.

Then, with the noon sight, the first inkling of uncertainty permeated through the boat. My calculations put our latitude sixty miles north of the dead reckoning position. I worked and re-worked through the almanac without success. Dave checked through the figures and still failed to confirm our D.R. position. I did not want to accept the truth and dismissed the noon sight as an inept sextant reading. But with Dave's afternoon sight my guarded doubts were confirmed. *Gipsy Moth* was definitely sixty miles further north than

our estimate. It was a great blow to morale, especially to mine. From thoughts of certain victory, it now seemed unlikely that we would outpace the larger boats in our class on handicap. How could such an error happen? The explanation was simple: *Gipsy Moth*'s log over-read by $5\frac{1}{2}$ per cent and with an overcast sky we had navigated entirely by dead reckoning from Cape Finisterre.

To make matters worse, the wind continued to decrease. By midnight we lay totally becalmed, suffering the incessant cacophony of spars, rigging and sails slatting in the swell. Even Garfunkel, our ace light weather helmsman, could make nothing of it. At the end of his watch he leapt into his bunk without a word. A gloomy voice, barely audible through the cocooning sleeping bag, remarked, 'We've spent four hours sailing four hundred yards in a complete circle.'

Throughout the following day and night, progress, although not quite so poor, continued to be unremarkable. Then, from my bunk, at the pre-dawn change of watch, I overheard a discussion from the deck *vis-a-vis* two horizontal red lights drawing nearer on the starboard quarter. Opinions varied as to the nature of the ship carrying them. The watch on thought it was probably a Dago fishing boat, while the relieving watch deduced that since a vessel carrying explosives shows one red light a vessel showing two must be carrying hydrogen bombs. Eventually Dave called me on deck for my opinion. By the time I reached the cockpit, 'Hawkeye' Clive had spotted red and green navigation lights and we were able to identify the approaching vessel as a sailing ship carrying red lights at her masthead to warn off low-flying aircraft.

But if the ship was sailing, how could she overhaul us at such incredible speed, we wondered. Our instruments showed an apparent wind coming from aft of three to four knots and *Gipsy Moth* was making just over three knots through the water. Yet here was a fully-rigged barque a hundred times heavier than *Gipsy Moth* overtaking at what we estimated to be seven or eight knots: it was unbelievable. Dave rushed down to listen through the hull with the transmit/receive loudhailer. 'Engine, I can hear a motor', he said, confirming our suspicion. The barque swept by leaving us in astonished agitation.

At dawn, which came soon afterwards, we saw *Tovarishch*, now sailing slightly slower than we were, about two miles ahead. We gradually overtook, and passed her by early afternoon just as the Selvagen Islands appeared on the horizon.

The Selvagen Islands until then had been specks on the chart which might easily have been mistaken for mildew. In reality, they were much bigger than expected. I was anxious to give them a wide berth; despite their size, they were unlit by a lighthouse and could become an embarrassment in the fading light. Nervous thoughts were erased when at last we found a soldier's wind from the northeast and sailed clear of the islands before last light. The wind held to take us round Tenerife's northeastern tip and on to Santa Cruz by mid-morning. *Gipsy Moth* crossed the line 9 days 22 hours and 23 minutes out from Plymouth. She was first to finish in her class.

After days of our own company, it was strange to be surrounded by other boats and many people. We had little time to become philosophical about it before John

The prize-giving at Tenerife: one of Zew Morza's *crew looking highly pleased.*

Dyson from Liptons U.K. and Pedro Duque who, among many other enterprises, is Liptons' agent in Tenerife, whisked us off for lunch in one of Pedro's limousines. His fleet became a source of bewilderment to us during our stay, when a day seldom passed without some new creation from the upper echelons of the international motor trade appearing. His generosity in their use never failed, and we were invariably transported in luxury to which we were unaccustomed.

Our arrival celebrations that evening stretched even Pedro's commodious vehicle (loaned to John Dyson for the occasion). Eight people fitted in quite neatly at the sober beginning of things, but this was quite beyond us for the return journey. The problem was finally resolved by packing a particularly comatose crew member into the boot.

An excursion the following day to 'El Teide', Tenerife's 12,000 ft volcano, did nothing to improve Clive's condition. The taxi and cable car ride were undemanding, but we were obliged to scrabble up the final 600 yards. In that distance we learned the meaning of a palpitating head and the previous evening became a painful memory. Our pain was nothing compared to Clive's, who turned the colour of the ashen surroundings and wisely gave up the summit attempt. The remainder in the party followed John Dyson, who encouraged us to the top waving his Lipton pennant. Our endeavours were rewarded by a magnificent view and fresh air, which in its purity at that altitude felt like icicles on my nicotine polluted lungs.

Back at Santa Cruz the fleet arrived at irregular intervals. Class A and larger Class B vessels docked near the town centre while yachts berthed in the fishing harbour outside the city limits. *G.B. II* welcomed arrivals with 'What shall we do with the drunken

Eendracht's crew spots Kruzenshtern during the cruise in company in the Canaries.

sailor?' and 'Rule Britannia', leaving her comparatively unimpeded by yachts wishing to make fast alongside.

The appearance of sewing machines on the quay from boats lucky enough to possess them marked the beginning of a gentle maintenance period in which crews swapped their stories and shared their technical expertise. Most boats appeared to need minor sail repairs and even those with major work were obliged to sort it out themselves. (The nearest sailmaker lived in Barcelona.) Rosemary and Minke sewed away on *Gipsy Moth's* sails, making good the temporary patches accumulated during the race. The rest of us worked on routine maintenance and preparation for the next leg. Somewhere in the general upheaval John Dyson left for England to pursue the serious aspects of his work. We missed him: in a short time he had become the eighth member of *Gipsy Moth's* crew.

The S.T.A. convened a meeting to hear my protest against *Tovarishch* and also that from another skipper

Christian Radich (left), and Regina Maris *with the Polish yacht* Hetman *off Tenerife.*

who surmised that she had motored on three separate occasions in the vicinity of his vessel. The committee found in favour of *Tovarishch*, waiving the protests as conjecture rather than certainty. The S.T.A.'s position was unenviable. My hope was that the protest would serve as a reminder to the Russian ship in the next race.

The rigmarole of protesting was soon forgotten in communal life at the fishing harbour. Days passed in work and idle chatter with our neighbours *Stortebeker* and *Polonez*. Nights were filled with things to eat, places to see, and people to meet. Social commitments gradually superceded the work load, and however enjoyable these were, solitude became a pressing need. We sailed for Gomero, a sparsely inhabited island southwest of Tenerife. Flukey winds and an overriding wish to take it easy made me decide to spend a quiet night at anchor in San Christianos before sailing on to Gomero.

The weather pattern with wind funnelling between the islands was unusual. Morning winds until just before noon were light and variable, then at around 11.30 the northeast trades rushed in at about force 6 or 7. This occurred on our crossing to Gomero. From soporific sunbathing in light airs to the need for a frantic sail reduction happened in the time it took to reach the foredeck. Later that day, during the return passage to San Christianos, the wind disappeared with similar speed, delaying our reunion with the fleet now gathered at Los Christianos for a beano to clinch the cruise in company and crew interchange.

This peculiar weather pattern recurred for the return passage to Santa Cruz. Vessels which motored early in the day arrived back before sunset, but those that dallied in the balmy conditions were later faced with strong headwinds and along with *Gipsy Moth* spent the night at sea.

In the day or two that remained before the start of the second leg, Caroline and I revictualled *Gipsy Moth* and collected the crew's laundry, which filled a taxi. Dave and I went to the skippers' meeting followed by a communications briefing where the race instructions and radio schedules were discussed.

A goodbye lunch of traditional suckling pig with Pedro and his friends, a last meander through the streets in Santa Cruz, a farewell party on board: then sleep for the following day.

Race 2 – Tenerife to Bermuda

Where the first leg had been something of a work-up to iron out *Gipsy Moth*'s little foibles, the second trans-atlantic race was the one which I hoped to win on handicap as well as taking line honours. In *Gipsy Moth* we had as near perfect a yacht as we could wish, specifically designed to race over the passage she was about to make. The race also introduced an additional attraction over the first leg tactics. Whereas the run from Plymouth to Tenerife had been a straightforward sail south which needed only a minor element of common sense in planning, the course to Bermuda required careful consideration.

The direct route to Bermuda is a distance of 2,517 miles but sailing the shortest distance does not necessarily mean the quickest passage. A yacht must take a course which will provide wind to fill her sails. She must search for the wind, and having found it endeavour to stay with it in order to arrive at her destination.

The navigator deciding a course need not rely entirely on his own knowledge to find those advantageous wind streams. They are recorded in various publications which base their data on observations made by ships using the established trading routes. Hence the trade winds, westerlies, doldrums et al came by the names which to the sailor describe their function. The Germans were probably the first to collate their sailing data into a readily available form to assist sailing ship masters in choosing the fastest and safest route to take. P Line nitrate trading ships using the *Segelhandbüch*, or an earlier version of it compiled for the use of the company's masters, recorded a far better cargo tonnage/time ratio than the British ships. They, with each captain jealously guarding his knowledge, recorded individually brilliant passage times but by and large the gross annual return was less efficient.

From the Routeing Chart it was obvious that a straight course for Bermuda was out of the question; it led through a high pressure area where the weather predictions indicated an above average likelihood of

Sagres and Juan Sebastian de Elcano *with* Kruzenshtern *astern, after the start of the second race (facing page).*

Libertad off Tenerife in the long ocean swell.

calms. It was advisable to take a southerly course where steadier winds were predicted. The trial of nerve came in deciding how far south to go: the further one went the better the wind, but it also added distance, so some compromise was essential. The second and far more important decision was when, having partially crossed the Atlantic, to turn north again. Some degree of light weather was unavoidable according to the Routeing Chart, but turning north too soon would result in excessive calms, and turning too late in excessive distance. Every navigator or skipper had a similar choice to make, although the ships equipped with weather chart facsimile receivers may have had some advantage over other competitors. High frequency radio also enabled others to receive forecasts from shore stations. Whether or not ships so equipped gained from their

superior electrical gear is doubtful. Correct interpretation is a major factor in the successful use of weather reports, and in unstable conditions interpretation calls for luck as well as skill.

The start at Tenerife inspired few competitors to attempt brilliant getaways. Time penalties for crossing the line before the gun and failing to restart were tough. It was possible, with a long line, for a yacht to start prematurely and be unaware that she had done so. This had happened to *Gefion* and *Polonez* at Plymouth, giving them several hours added on their corrected times. Against the risk of such a penalty, a few minutes lost at the beginning seemed relatively unimportant in a race of two to three thousand miles.

An exception to this general lack of urgency was *Kruzenshtern*, which having taken a long leg out to sea bore down on the line in spectacular and perfectly timed style. She came unstuck just before the line, when I think she confused a spectator craft with the official starting vessel marking the outer limit. As a result she crossed outside the line and was obliged to hand sail, motor back, rehoist her canvas and begin again.

Opinions varied over the best course to clear Tenerife and its associated unstable winds. *Dar Pormoza* led roughly half the fleet close inshore taking advantage of the breeze funnelling down from the hills. In *Dar Pormoza*'s case this paid off. Hugging the coast, she appeared to find private winds which took her into a clear lead. Luck may have played some part in this, but I doubt it. Captain Jurkiewicz had served on board since 1931 and it is reasonable to assume that his skill and that of his officers and crew put *Dar Pormoza* ahead. For us, as spectators to her progress, it was a rare experience to see a full-rigged ship wriggling along the coast looking for wind slants.

The remaining vessels sailed out to sea where theoretically the wind would be less affected by Tenerife's landmass. By and large, this was the best course to take, although even well out there was little wind to speak of until much later when strong cyclonic gusts passed through the gap between Tenerife and Hierro. Playing each wind shift as it came, we were uncertain for some time whether to pass north or south of Hierro. A steadier than usual slant finally pushed us south.

As soon as we had cleared the islands the northeast trades set in. *Gipsy Moth* responded with her usual alacrity and charged off. She was a delight to sail, mirroring with her measured reaction to wind and sea my own sense of freedom and joy at independence from the land.

Peter Hambly

In the first two days *Gipsy Moth* raced to the limit of her maximum theoretical hull speed of 8.7 knots. However gratifying this was, it did nothing to make good the two hours a day we had to give *Gladan* in order to win on handicap. I used *Gladan* as a yardstick since she was, judging from her last performance, *Gipsy Moth*'s nearest rival. Though *Sir Winston Churchill* had actually won our class on handicap, I thought it unlikely that she could seriously challenge *Gladan* in a prolonged tactical situation. Garfunkel and I worked to a theory that if *Gipsy Moth* sailed at $6\frac{1}{2}$ knots using all available wind, *Gladan*'s relative speed, considering her size and weight, would drop accordingly, giving us the edge. My impression was that our steering was below par, so I set about throwing a minor tantrum whenever the helmsman deviated from the course. This was a private game I contrived to improve the general helming standard.

Later, even though ability had passed beyond reasonable expectations, I continued to harangue the helmsman for the slightest inattention. It was the only real discipline ever imposed on board and paid enormous dividends in the calms ahead.

On May 26 with the speedo reading the magical $6\frac{1}{2}$ knots we spotted *Dar Pormoza* several miles ahead on a similar course. *Gipsy Moth* slowly overhauled and drew ahead by mid-afternoon. Some sixty miles due north of us *Kukri*, a British Army sloop, broke her wheel steering gear. The crew rigged the emergency tiller to sail back to Tenerife where a new steering gear, flown out from England, waited her arrival. *Kukri* set off again within nine hours of her arrival in Tenerife.

From the positions reported on the morning radio schedule, tactical patterns were beginning to emerge. The square-riggers, sailing with the main body of the fleet including ourselves, had chosen a middle route south. *Churchill* appeared to be making for a lower latitude; *Sabre, Polonez* and *Endraacht* were slightly north, leaving *Glénan* out on a limb even further north. *Gladan* was on exactly the same track as *Gipsy Moth* but some miles ahead. We caught her up the following afternoon. At last our greatest rival was within hailing distance. As the sun set, so the wind dropped with it. Providence seemed to be smiling. In light airs a big schooner couldn't hope to compete against *Gipsy Moth*. That night we slept the sleep of the fulfilled and in the grey light of pre-dawn an empty horizon greeted a casual lookout. Hawkeye Clive went up to peer around. His gaze swept through a full arc, then returned to port. 'Sail fine on the port bow. It's a schooner – dammit, it's *Gladan*!'

I swore and cursed at everything in general and at the S.T.A. in particular. How could we possibly make up the two hours a day *Gipsy Moth* had to give *Gladan* when the Swedish schooner sailed like a dream in light airs? As the two boats drifted level again my rantings at the S.T.A. rating formula became so much nonsense. *Gladan* was sailed beautifully; her crew moved around the decks quickly, yet gently to avoid upsetting the sails' precarious balance in light airs. Sheets were eased and hardened in to allow for the faintest windshift. We tried our damnedest to pass clear ahead and in ten hours managed a mere two boat lengths. Then fate, abetted by Dave's nose for these things, took a decisive hand in our favour. Both boats lay totally becalmed within two hundred yards of each other when a suggestion of a breeze puffed from the southwest. *Gladan* and *Gipsy Moth* tacked towards the south where the Pilot Charts predicted stronger winds. After a few moments chart-gazing Dave, who was on watch at the time, decided that a southwest wind was a local anomaly and our course, leading away from our objective Bermuda, was illogical. Dave's watch put the boat about and we continued to trickle along with our private zephyr while *Gladan* lay becalmed.

We were off again, with only seventy miles separating us from the favourite for line honours, *Great Britain II*. There was no hope of catching her, but with no other boat between us we had every reason to be cheerful.

Life on board was tranquil. The watch system of four hour stints at night and six hours during the day worked well. A six hour stretch allowed the watch below a reasonable sleep or, if they couldn't do that, time to do whatever they chose. Two watches of three people left the seventh hand free for domestic duties. 'Cook day', as these duties were called, came up in strict rotation giving everyone a complete break from normal routine. The working watches had a constant servant re-

Gladan, *by now perceived as a strong competitor to* Gipsy Moth.

peculiar results, though eventually we got the knack. But no matter how adept we became, breadmaking of all the tasks on board remained the only real chore.

'Drink' drinks at six sharp were an important ritual, a time when the volume went up on the tape recorder and we sat chatting in the cockpit until just before supper when the girls metamorphosed from bikinis into long dresses. This may seem like an affectation and perhaps it was, but their elegant appearance for dinner on a small yacht hundreds of miles from anywhere was something special and good for everyone's morale.

The comfort of our domestic life belied and yet helped the business of sailing *Gipsy Moth*. We took infinite pains to gain a minute increase in speed. A watch never went by without some sail adjustment being made, and constant attention to sail trim meant a definite improvement in performance. Nothing we could do was left undone and in Bermuda we knew, regardless of results, that we had sailed her to the limit of our ability.

While we delighted in our good fortune, the major part of the fleet made slow progress. *Tina IV* became the honorary radio relay station for vessels that could not contact *Sir Winston Churchill* direct. Morning radio schedules, after the formal business of position reporting was over, became a chat period when the generous swapped weather information and generally passed the time of day with other competitors. *G.B. II* sailed outside radio reception range from *Churchill* and we set up a private schedule with *G.B. II* to relay her daily positions. In turn, they with their high frequency transmitter contacted Rosemary's parents to send on her smallpox vaccination certificate which she had forgotten.

In light airs the square-rigged ships and heavily built

sponsible not only for cooking and washing up but also for keep *Gipsy Moth* clean and uncluttered. What to cook was given much thought with everyone taking special care over the main evening meal. Specialities evolved, ranging from beautifully prepared salads to continental potroasts. Wonders were produced on the two-burner paraffin (kerosene) stove. Fresh bread was baked daily in a large biscuit type tin oven designed to fit over the burners. Early attempts in this field produced

Baltic traders made slow progress. Brian Watson, skippering *Lindø*, was first to decide that unless he motored *Lindø* had little chance of arriving in Bermuda in time for the third leg. He officially retired and started her engine. *Kruzenshtern*, becalmed at night near another competitor, a sloop, switched her lights off. The sloop's skipper, puzzled by such behaviour, turned his Aldis lamp on the ship to see what had happened; *Kruzenshtern* immediately switched her navigation lights back on again. The two vessels repeated this performance four times within the next hour until *Kruzenshtern*, presumably tiring of the game, turned her lights off and disappeared!

When the fleet finally cleared the calms *G.B. II* retained a clear lead. *Gipsy Moth* was a few miles further west than *Stella Polare* and three hundred miles ahead of *Gladan*. We had reached the latitude (24°30′S) on which we had planned to run down our westing.

An expanse of ocean may seem dauntingly barren but there were countless things of interest. Seabirds were frequent visitors. A pair of Bermudan longtails invariably circled *Gipsy Moth* at dawn and flew off again. We became superstitious about them, greeting their appearance as an omen for good sailing. Magical qualities were also attributed to porpoises, though without the conviction bestowed on our longtails. Flying fish leapt on board occasionally but never in sufficient numbers to make an impression on our diet.

In our isolation particular incidents assumed importance. A moment's inattention by Rosemary at the helm sent *Gipsy Moth* careering broadside to the sea. A wave sluiced through the forecabin skylight, drenching my sleeping bag. My annoyance was appeased the following day when I, similarly inattentive at the helm, allowed a wave through the main skylight. Of all the people sitting round the saloon table, Rosemary was singled out to receive the full impact.

A mystery which we never solved occurred during Garfunkel's trick at the helm. His claim that he could smell something burning sent us scurrying round the boat looking for a possible source. Finding nothing, we dismissed it to his over-active imagination. 'I tell you I can smell something burning', Garfunkel persisted. We ignored him until a little later when the T-shirt draped round his neck burst into flames. God knows how it happened.

Our only medical concern arose from heat exhaustion. Caroline was a determined sunbather, inclined to drink less than the average daily intake. Perhaps this tendency was magnified by a loose form of water rationing instigated as an extra precaution in the early calms. Whatever the cause, Caroline suffered badly until a ban from sunbathing, salt tablets and forced feeding of a gallon of water a day cured the complaint. Apart from my overriding concern for her health, there was also a feeling that we, the crew, were essential cogs in *Gipsy Moth*'s machinery and that the 'weakest link in the chain' adage applied.

After four days making our westing the time came to reach towards the north. *Stella Polare* had passed during the previous day on a course obviously inclined towards the north, and we had reached the pencil mark on the chart where back in Tenerife the decision to turn had been made. For two days *Gipsy Moth* continued at well above Chichester's target of 200 miles a day. Then our speed dropped to 180, then 84 miles, then we were becalmed. The high pressure area had allowed *Great Britain II* and *Stella Polare* to scrape past before it moved southwest. We were trapped.

Now came the real trial of the entire race. In order to

Sagres on passage between Tenerife and Bermuda.

win we had to get out of the calm before the other boats in our class caught up. *Gladan* and *Churchill* were still belting along on the trade winds, gaining at 10 knots an hour. *Zew Morza* was approaching fast from the east. We played the sheets, tacked, gybed, hoisted and lowered appropriate sails, and fretted over the first radio schedule in our new situation. Would the others be caught like *Gipsy Moth*, or would we stay becalmed like a lame duck while the sailed past? By his tone, *Churchill*'s captain gave no indication of untoward unhappiness as he opened the schedule. Our hopes sank.

We renewed our efforts and I gained the enmity of everyone on board by insisting on gybes, counter gybes and complete sail changes. In twenty-four hours we logged twenty-two miles making good eleven miles towards Bermuda. Then came the radio schedule. *Churchill* opened up sounding wonderfully depressed. 'Gentlemen, I have had it put to me that in view of these persistent calms I should ask the Race Committee whether they could consent to finishing the race at sea. This is a possibility I foresaw ten days ago in the last calm and I warned my "Lords and Masters" that unless the wind improved this might become a necessity. I will ask your individual views at the end of the schedule.'

The general response was one of agreement leaving only a few boats determined to see the race through. *Polonez* naturally wanted to carry on. *Stortebeker* observed a discreet radio silence. *Gladan* pretended not to understand what was going on and beavered away at sailing to Bermuda. I adopted what I thought was a suitably conciliatory tone and pointed out that the lead boats were through the calm and could not be expected to welcome a finish at sea which would in the circumstances give a time advantage to those vessels that had yet to sail through it. Captain Collis thought the situation had transgressed the win-or-lose concept and was now one of survival. I thought that no vessel, after only fifteen days at sea, should be in a survival situation.

The drama began in earnest on the following day when the S.T.A. Committee in their wisdom ruled that the race should go on, stressing that any vessel wishing to retire could do so. *Churchill* set about getting the fuel and water state of every vessel in the fleet, presumably to help a rescue operation should the need occur. This misled at least one ship into thinking a fellow competitor required assistance. *Lindø*, with enough water on board for everyone to have least a shower a day, heard *Polonez* report the quantity she had and assumed they needed help. *Lindø* set off on her errand and eventually found *Polonez* drifting peacefully along. Chris Baranowski was astonished at the offer of water and declined; he passed across a bottle of vodka in thanks for *Lindø*'s intentions.

That's not to say *Polonez*' crew weren't concerned by the calm: they were. Polish sea superstition is as rich in lore as any maritime nation and Chris delved for traditional wind bringers. A bottle of vodka thrown to Zeus failed to stir the gods. *Polonez*'s last hope lay with the beautiful Mona who had 'hitched' the Atlantic crossing. Poland's mythology claims that, as a last and infallible measure, a virgin scraping the mast heel with her fingernails 'will bring tempest from calm'. Mona was set to work. Twenty-four hours later the crew on *Polonez* were either bemused or had lost faith in one of their country's traditions. *Carillion of Wight* from the Christian Sailing Centre at Cowes sought wind by the more orthodox expedient of prayer. Some vessels retired. Most carried on.

It is difficult for anyone who has not experienced a prolonged calm to understand the misery of it. Slatting sails, the jarring crack as spars swinging wildly in the swell reach their restraining point, the feeling of dead weight as the transom belly-flops into troughs. These are part of it: worse still is the lonely feeling born from helplessness. The ship will not – cannot – respond and in losing drive it loses its life. Without wind it is useless. This rubs off onto the crew, who at first accept their predicament philosophically, believing wind will come. When it doesn't, morale plummets making mincemeat of the spirit. Then effort begins to count a lot.

Our third day was the worst. A faint unconvincing breeze came before dawn and died as the sun rose. Throughout the morning *Gipsy Moth*'s log quivered between 0 and 0.3 knots. By noon, the heat on deck was unbearable; tricks at the helm were reduced to ten minutes. Sail changes, which in normal conditions had become automatic procedures similar to changing gear in a car, now called for determination. Spirits flagged, so we dropped the sails and dived in for a swim. The first minutes were luxurious, but imagination quickly dawned to make cowards of us. The swim served its purpose: it was a turning point, giving back some of our former zest in sail handling. The heat seemed less oppressive and the time to sunset passed quickly.

At dawn the longtails circled. *Gipsy Moth*'s sails filled, stirring the dormant speedo which crept up the scale, lingered at 1.5 knots, then carried on climbing. Bermuda lay 184 miles northwest.

Eight hundred miles back, *Zenobe Gramme* took *Kukri* and *Erika* in tow. The German Navy's barque *Gorch Fock*, on passage to Bermuda independently from the S.T.A. fleet, stopped for twenty-four hours to assist any vessel that required help. *Master Builder* took advantage of this by arranging a rendezvous for additional fuel. With diesel to spare, *Builder* motored on

Zenobe Gramme *towing* Kukri, *and later* Erika *as well during the calms.*

to replenish *Outlaw*. Of the forty-one vessels in the race, sixteen retired. According to a dour European captain who commanded a large Bermudan ketch, *Tovarishch* resolved the dilemma differently. He commented laconically, 'When I try in light airs, it is possible to sail my ship 45°, maybe 40°, to the wind. When I see *Tovarishch* overtaking me at 35° to the wind, I think it unusual.'

Bermuda is a small archipelago with few distinguishing features to navigate by. Our approach from SSE left the finishing mark, St David's lighthouse, obscure until twenty-five minutes before we crossed. I reported *Gipsy Moth*'s E.T.A. to Bermuda Radio when St David's became visible and they passed the information on. The first person we saw after passing through the narrows at St George's Harbour was Henry Dallas, perched on the foredeck of a small hired launch clutching the most thoughtful gift imaginable – a case of refrigerated beer. Henry's company, as far as we could tell, imported a fair share of Bermuda's food requirements and one of his business interests was the agency for Lipton's Tea. Our stay in Bermuda was to be a holiday exceeding all expectations, due mainly to Henry and his family's hospitality.

The greatest surprise as we entered the inner harbour was to see *Stortebeker* made fast alongside. Her skipper Hanns Temme had reported their position irregularly throughout the passage, claiming 'generator problems'. I never managed to draw Hanns on whether or not his generator problems were a tactical exercise to keep *Stortebeker*'s progress out of the limelight. The most I ever got from him was a radiant smile whenever the subject cropped up. Hanns sailed a spectacular race, heading south after the first calm despite protest from his crew. At 22°N latitude, much further south than any

Del Rio *and* Serena, *owned by Henry and Mollie Dallas, and their son Steve.*

Bermuda 14-footers racing.

other competitors, they found strong and steady trade winds to carry her along the latitude. I was ecstatic about *Stortebeker*'s performance and at their tenacity in going south. Although justifiably pleased with the outcome, Hanns remarked humbly, 'But don't you have a *Segelhandbüch* in England? It illustrates quite clearly that the conditions we experienced were for normal July weather not for May. That is why I went south.' Unfortunately *Stortebeker* was disqualified by the rule which requires at least half the crew to be under age twenty-five. Everyone on board knew this was inevitable before they left Tenerife, which allayed the disappointment they might have felt. The S.T.A. kindly published the results list including those who had infringed this rule, and appropriately noted their disqualification. *Stortebeker* would have been placed second to *Stella Polare* in the spinnaker class, with *G.B. II* third.

In her class *Gipsy Moth* had finished first, but the result on handicap remained open until other competitors crossed the line or the race time limit expired. The Time Correction Factor gave *Gladan* two and a half days: if she arrived within that time, the race was hers. The same, with adjustment for T.C.F., applied to any other vessel in *Gipsy Moth*'s class, but my paranoia lay with *Gladan*.

Race results were far from our minds as we secured alongside *Stortebeker*. John Hamilton, who was responsible for the S.T.A. satellite office at St George's, came on board with *Stortebeker*'s crew to give us a tremendous welcome. The press and television people clamoured around, and Henry with his wife Molly paced up and down the quay periodically shouting the most welcome invitation, 'Come on kids, I've booked a table for lunch.' It was strange to be with different people again. The grunts and mumbles which in our confined sphere had passed for articulate conversation were now inadequate for normal use.

In the next days we came to understand how Bermuda had built its reputation as a holiday island. From St George's we sailed south to moor at the Royal Bermuda Yacht Club in Hamilton, the capital. Steve Dallas, Henry's son, became a regular companion and friend who delighted in showing us the island and especially the surrounding sea which he loved. His passion was game fishing. It always gives me pleasure to watch someone of ability and Steve excelled in his pursuits. He understood the fishes' habits, could pilot his boat with ease through reef-strewn passages to get to them, and best of all had a great sense of conservation about the whole business. Steve told the story of a tourist who regularly visited the island to fish. Apparently this man hired an air-conditioned charter boat festooned with rods and outriggers to set off daily for the fishing grounds with two locals who knew their way about. One of these steered while the other tended the rods. Meanwhile the charter guest sat waiting in air-conditioned isolation sipping whisky. The trio swanned about like this until the rod man hooked a fish. He then yelled 'Strike!' at which the whisky sipper leapt from his emporium to play the creature.

Spear-fishing, a favourite pastime of mine, was something else that Steve excelled in. He had that uncanny knack of by passing what seemed to me perfect reefs, in favour of isolated outcrops that naturally abounded in fish. We caught enough to feed his family and everyone on *Gipsy Moth*.

On our third day at Hamilton, Roger Bonnett came out from the U.K. to join the crew. There was no permanent berth for him so he and Clive set about making the forepeak sail storage compartment into a habitable area. It was good to have someone new join us, although Roger may have found it odd settling into a well established introversive group. He barely had time to unpack his swimming trunks before Steve arrived to take everyone off for an afternoon's tuition in water skiing. It was fun, and we all learned to a greater or lesser degree how to stay upright. That is all except Caroline, who persistently bounced on her right buttock.

So life went on. Most mornings Henry woke us with a 'Hi kids, need some more ice?' Days were filled with a variety of aquatic pursuits. Evenings were spent with friends ashore, on board and on other boats. Dave and Minke hired a moped to see the island. (Mopeds are a popular means of transport in a land with a 25 m.p.h. speed limit and where the sun shines.) We watched the Bermuda fourteen foot dinghies racing – incredible craft carrying as much as a thousand square feet of canvas.

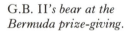

G.B. II's *bear at the Bermuda prize-giving.*

We spent a day as guests on board Dar Pormoza.

Meanwhile the time limit for the Tenerife to Bermuda race expired. The S.T.A. had a special clause in their rules to allow for vessels which had not crossed the line at the given time. Rule 30 ran as follows:

All Sail Training Races unless specified to the contrary in Sailing Instructions will have a time limit and the time of the end of each race will be published in Sailing Instructions for the race.

Elapsed times of vessels which have not crossed the finishing line by the time limit will be calculated from the formula:

$$\text{Elapsed Time} = T \times \left(\frac{D}{D-d} + \frac{0.2d}{D} \right)$$

D = the length of course as published in Sailing Instructions.
d = the distance of the vessel from the finishing line at the time limit.
T = the time from the start of the race to the time limit.

From this, and with the positions given by vessels on the time limit, Dave set to work with his calculator. He ran through the list gradually whittling down the boats that seriously threatened our time until only one remained to be checked out: *Gladan.* Dave laboured with infinite care, re-checked his figures with deliberation, and finally announced, 'I reckon we've won by fifty-nine minutes.' His calculations were confirmed two days later by the S.T.A.'s official results.

Race 3 – Bermuda to Newport, Rhode Island

To understand the mêlée at the beginning of the Bermuda to Newport race, we must go back to the captains' briefing in Bermuda. At this meeting Captain von Stackelberg, *Gorch Fock*'s master, suggested a special amendment for Class A ships (square-rigged) of the S.T.A. rule which required engines to be stopped on the preparatory signal. Captain Stackelberg held the view that the starting line, close to Bermuda's northern reefs, was short and might prove dangerous in adverse winds. To overcome this possibility he proposed that square-rigged vessels should be allowed to use their engines up to the line. The S.T.A. put the motion to a vote, which was carried. Someone, I think it was von Stackelberg, said that besides any other consideration, a close start would provide a spectacle.

Spectacle it was. Eighteen square-riggers under sail, some charging with engines on full ahead to the windward end of the line, made an unbelievable sight. 'Was Trafalgar as good as this, do you suppose?' and, 'I've seen dinghies starting further apart on a gravel pit,' were comments I recollect. Afterwards, we heard about the collisions.

Erewan, an undercanvassed barquentine registered in Panama, sailing perfectly within her rights, inadvertently caused all three collisions simply through engine failure. In the dash to the line *Erewan*'s engine stalled. With her limited sail area she quickly lost speed, thereby baulking the vessels coming up behind. *Mircea*, sailing on a course perpendicular to the start line, overran and dismasted *Gazela Primeiro* which was attempting to avoid *Erewan*. *Gazela Primeiro* was then forced into *Christian Radich*, which, with foresight, avoided severe impact by clewing up her royals and topgallants. The major collision occurred between *Libertad* and *Juan Sebastian de Elcano*. *Libertad*, sailing full and by more or less along the starting line, bore down on *Juan Sebastian*. Flanked by *Sagres* (with her engines going astern to avoid *Erewan*) to starboard, and by the Columbian barque *Gloria* to port, *Juan Sebastian* could not take evasive action. With

a collision in the offing, she too put her engines full astern. But *Libertad* held her course even after Captain Nalda had hailed the Argentine vessel to turn to starboard. *Juan Sebastian* finally turned more to port but could not avoid striking *Libertad*'s port quarter. Her bowsprit snapped off carrying the topmast forestay with it. The topmast held momentarily, then toppled forward pitching Benito Sanz from the topgallant yard. He was saved from certain death by the lower topsail yard, which broke his fall and held him until helpers lowered him to the deck, seriously injured.

Gazela Primeiro and *Juan Sebastian de Elcano* retired to Bermuda for temporary repairs. Both vessels were able to rejoin the fleet in time for the Hudson River Parade of Sail. After an official protest meeting at Newport, *Libertad* was disqualified.

Another, more lighthearted, collision occurred at the Class B Division II start. *Stella Polare*, with her spinnaker pole rigged lying ready to go on the pulpit, used it to punch a four-inch hole in the side of H.M.S. *Eskimo*, the start ship. Stories differ how this happened: some say that *Stella Polare* was forced onto *Eskimo* by two outside yachts. Others reckon *Stella Polare*'s mainsheet jammed and she was unable to bear off. What everyone does agree on is Captain Faggioni's reaction. 'Today,' he said, 'I have achieved what I was unable to do throughout the war. I have holed a British warship.'

Our start in Division I was more leisurely, with Rosemary and Garfunkel sitting on deck casually repairing the No. 1 jib which had torn on the way to the starting line. We had no preconceived ambitions for this race, chiefly because we badly needed a rest after the Bermuda holiday. Something of our former zeal returned when *Maruffa* passed with a vocal flourish. Had they gone by without provocation, I doubt whether

we would have bothered. As it was, a winch handle appeared in Clive's hand and Minke stood by to tail, all unrehearsed, in deliberate silence. The race was on. We sat on *Maruffa*'s tail slowly closing the distance. They seemed determined not to let *Gipsy Moth* by, forcing us to resort to subterfuge. We paid off occasionally to give the impression that we would overtake politely to leeward and *Maruffa* responded predictably, paying off the wind to baulk our intention. The ploy carried on until a minor habit was established. Then, feeling the time was right, we went through the established motions with *Maruffa* following suit. At the last moment our helm went down, sheets came in and we passed her to windward.

By the time that little tussle was over *Gipsy Moth* was abeam of *Dar Pormoza*. We dipped the ensign and cheered. They followed suit, cheering and waving from the deck and from the ratlines. A camaraderie had developed between the crews who had sailed all the way from Plymouth.

The next vessel we drew level with was the U.S. Coast Guard's barque *Eagle*. After the New York Parade of Sail I have every reason to admire the efficiency of the Coast Guards and can understand the pride men of that service feel for their emblem. Seeing it embossed on a sailing ship was a bit surreal. Rumours were that a cost-conscious government department was thinking of dispensing with *Eagle*: if painting the emblem on the side in some way retains her in service, then I'm all for it, but if it is only a bureaucratic whim I wish they would reconsider.

Soon after we had passed *Eagle* the wind dropped, sunset came and throughout the night we saw bobbing lights from various competitors around the horizon. In the early morning light *Gorch Fock* appeared a little off to port. We spent the day sailing in company and finally lost her when the wind became even lighter.

Dave had a gift for finding wind. Whether this was instinct or calculation I never discovered. I did learn to take his mildest notion that it might be advisable to go in such a such direction seriously. That night in failing winds he suggested a more westerly course. Sure enough, on the following day's radio link we heard that the major part of the fleet was becalmed. *Gipsy Moth*, still sailing, lay second to *Ticonderoga* in our class. This surprised us and put enthusiasm back into our efforts, despite the certainty that *Ticonderoga* was, bar an accident, unbeatable.

The captain of Eagle *(left foreground) deliberately held his ship back from the crowded starting line and under very little sail; this kept her clear of the mêlée and able to make a reasonable start. The photograph on the left was taken from* Dar Pormoza*; to the left of H.M.S.* Eskimo *can be seen the damaged* Gazela Primeiro *in the midst of the bigger ships.*

Radio schedules on the Newport leg lost the importance attached to them in the previous races. The fleet now numbered eighty-four vessels, making the daily call up to *Bay States* (the communications ship) a long procedure. Also the large increase in the fleet (it had doubled in size) made the schedule less personal than it had been. Vessels that had joined in Bermuda were merely a name on a call-up list, rather than a known group of people. Perhaps what undermined the schedule's importance most of all was the comparatively short distance involved (600 miles). It was difficult to have that 'isolation seeking comfort in communication' feeling when there were eighty-three other boats around with another 160 yachts from the Newport to Bermuda Race approaching on a reciprocal course.

Tina IV kept the ball rolling with occasional post-schedule anecdotes. A classic came over the air when *Tina*, lying becalmed near *Gorch Fock*, requested a position check by *Gorch Fock*'s Omega navigation system. There was a long pause after the request while *Gorch Fock*'s wireless operator sought the captain's permission to relay the position. The German barque eventually came up with, 'I regret I cannot pass this information; it will reveal our tactics.' *Tina* whispered, 'But we're becalmed.'

Ghosting along towards the U.S.A.; Garfunkle sitting out, Roger Bonnett in the bows, Caroline steering. For evening drinks before watch change and dinner midway between Bermuda and Newport, the girls would change into long skirts.

With eight people on board *Gipsy Moth* the routine altered; we adopted a three watch system of two people per watch working a four hour stint. Cook day duties continued as before leaving the eighth hand on twenty-four hour standby to assist the watches whenever help was needed on deck. Cook day and standby worked in rotation, and compiling the rota for these tasks involved some fairly complicated juggling. Dave sorted it out amicably; everyone, in our 'cruising' frame of mind, welcomed the eight uninterrupted hours off which this system gave.

The Gulf Stream accounted for our return to a cruising mentality. In Bermuda the U.S. National Weather Service had thoughtfully briefed skippers on the intricacies of the Gulf Stream. We learned the jargon used by sailors crossing it regularly. Shelf water, slope water, and warm and cold eddies were factors in navigating the stream; water temperature, cloud formation and the sea's colour gave additional information for a successful passage. So with the textbook in one hand, thermometer in the other, Garfunkel set about guiding us across this unpredictable stretch of water. In theory it seemed simple; all you needed to do was use the north-going segment of a 'warm slope' to advantage. The Weather Service people had kindly provided a forecast chart showing an ideal slope and naturally we navigated for it. Unfortunately, by the time we arrived at the critical point the chart was three days out of date. Garfunkel leapt up and down with buckets of water for temperature readings. Hawkeye Clive consulted the horizon for desirable grey seas, and the girls went cloud-spotting. Then I accidentally threw the thermometer overboard. Careful sextant work by Dave on the next day put *Gipsy Moth* west and slightly back from her previous position. There was no doubt that we had found the Gulf Stream, but the wrong part. Our general attitude changed immediately from quiet determination to one of leisurely cruising.

The Class A ships making slow progress in light winds finished their race ahead of the allocated time limit. America waited to see the Tall Ships, and if they lay becalmed at sea the weekend crowds expected at Newport would either stay away or be disappointed. Financial considerations made it imperative that the public had their spectacle. It was a first inkling of the

commercial interest the Tall Ships Race would encounter. Some commercial enterprises rightly benefited the general Op Sail Fund which financed the U.S. programme; others did not. As a result of this and wishing to have some control over the quality of merchandising, the American Sail Training Association had registered as a world trademark the words 'Tall Ships' and a logo, making commercial users of these words liable to seek permission and pay a fee for use to the A.S.T.A. I've always considered tall ships an international affair and feel vaguely put out by such a fee, but presumably revenue gained in this way will help towards the cost of future American events.

The premature finish at sea worked against *Dar Pormoza*, which was tactically in the best position and had the race continued would probably have won. As it happened, *Gorch Fock* lay marginally nearer to Newport and got first place; *Dar Pormoza* came second.

A wind with strength in it drove *Gipsy Moth* on a fine reach towards her destination. Clearing the Gulf Stream into colder northern waters brought oilskins and sweaters from their lockers for the first time since Tenerife. Visibility deteriorated over the American continental shelf, bringing the usual anxiety for a landfall in such conditions. A short break in the fog enabled us to identify Block Island light off the tip of Long Island in the western approaches to Rhode Island Sound. We made the appropriate alteration in course and in the faint early morning breeze ghosted on to cross the finishing line.

Gipsy Moth's arrival preceded the Class A Ships by several hours, but already the Coast Guards were out in strength to control spectator craft and guide competitors to their berths. To our initial disappointment we were allocated a quay some distance from the centre

Dolphin in the Gulf Stream

The American schooner Shenandoah *(left), which although primarily employed on commercial summer cruises is used for sail training outside the season.* Esmeralda *with a Coast Guard escort as she sails into the anchorage at Newport (right).*

Bill of Rights, *also a famous cruise schooner which gives support and sea time to sail training (left).* Nippon Maru *at Newport (right); problems of distance and scheduling made it impossible for her to sail in the Tall Ships Race, but she did arrive from Japan in time for the Parade of Sail.*

of things, but this gave way to relief later in the day when we saw the crowds gathered round the Treadway Inn. *G.B. II* was moored there entertaining a vast audience with periodic renderings of 'Rule Britannia' and a new addition to their repertoire, 'Hip Hip Hooray'.

Newport astonished my preconceptions. Houses, mainly constructed in wood, lined cobbled streets. Huge cars cruised along the back streets with all the assurance of ocean liners. Armed policemen controlled the traffic. People, thousands of them in holiday regalia, thronged the pavements. Hamburgers and hotdogs, Tall Ships T-shirts and Tall Ships trinkets were available.

Americans welcomed the fleet to their Bicentennial celebrations with the hospitality for which their country is known in Europe. A special 'hospitality centre' for visiting cadets organized excursions, parties and general events. Skippers were dined and danced in the mansions built in Newport's heyday as a resort for the wealthy.

Stortebeker arrived two days after *Gipsy Moth*, having spent the interim becalmed in the vicinity of the Nantucket Light Vessel. Hann's tactical originality misfired on this occasion. There was an agreement between the two boats that whoever arrived first bought the beer, so *Gipsy Moth* happily coughed up with that and lunch as well. *Stortebeker*'s crew were great optimists in judging passage times and invariably spent the last days at sea eating hardtack. When they came to Newport they had the lean look of ship's biscuit-eaters. To eat and drink with them again was a great pleasure.

Another late arrival was *Sir Winston Churchill*. An all-female crew drew spectators in droves as the schooner came alongside at the Treadway Inn with the girls manning the yards. The main attraction for the

The Newport spectator fleet under the Goodyear airship.

Artillery men dressed in eighteenth century costumes fired their cannons, setting the Bicentennial tone. The highlight of the whole affair came when masters from the big ships presented Captain Jurkiewicz with an oil painting of his ship *Dar Pormoza*. It was a touching reminder that after the American celebrations, Captain Jurkiewicz would relinquish his command having spent some forty years rising from boy to captain on board.

Kruzenshtern *and* Nippon Maru *pass at Newport.*

general public, though, was naturally the square-riggers moored to buoys in the harbour: they were the focal point of the whole exercise. Fellow competitors in smaller boats had by then become a bit blasé about the ships. After that incredible start at Bermuda they had witnessed the greatest sight in recent sailing ship history. To see them moored together was charming but relatively tame.

We had planned to leave Newport early to visit some smaller ports in Long Island Sound, but news that *Gipsy Moth* had won a prize kept us back until the presentation day. Prancing young ladies, high-stepping in precision and marching to the sound of assorted bands, were the preamble to the event at Fort Adams.

The Parade of Sail

The American Sail Training Association organized the reception for vessels at Newport, Rhode Island to coincide with their coastal race. After Newport, Op Sail's various committees co-ordinated everything for the New York Parade of Sail and later out-port visits. What was to be the outstanding event of America's Bicentennial celebrations was gathering momentum. Hundreds of ships from all over the world converged on New York, all within a few hours' sail. What began in 1971 as the brainchild of Frank Braynard, Op Sail's General Manager, was about to materialize.

At Newport an operations manual for the whole performance was given to the skippers. It was a colossal tome produced with meticulous regard for detail which gave us an inkling of the effort that had been made to bring the ships together. Committees, sub-committees and committees to sub-committees had been formed to deal with contingencies ranging from the order of parade to free buns and bus passes in New York. The first phase from the manual outlined a plan to move the smaller vessels through Long Island Sound towards New York with two overnight stops before the actual parade. Meanwhile, vessels with masts too high to pass under the Brooklyn Bridge were to sail outside Long Island and rejoin the fleet at assorted anchorages near Staten Island. The combined fleet would then make its way up the Hudson, past the New Jersey shore and the west side of Manhattan.

Long Island Sound was the most fraught night navigation of our entire voyage. British Admiralty charts bought just before departure from England showed lights seldom bearing any resemblance to reality. Combined with poor visibility and a tight schedule, this made windward work along the Sound a demanding business. We resolved the problem by beating from shore to shore and tacking as the echo sounder showed twelve feet. At dawn we were able to re-establish our position.

Daytime sailing, although visibility remained indifferent, was much more fun. It seemed that anyone

New York's traditional fireboat welcome for great ships (left).

Hope, *believed to be the last oyster sloop built on Long Island Sound, and the Connecticut entry in the Parade of Sail.*

when Giles Chichester and his friends Brian and Sue joined us. It's a bit unnerving to have the part-owner of any boat join the crew, but doubly so with *Gipsy Moth*. We needn't have worried: Giles and his friends easily slipped into the way of life on board and contributed a lot to the general enjoyment.

The next phase in the operation was to rendezvous at Execution Rock at the inner end of Long Island Sound with our group for passage through Hell Gate, down the East River and then to an anchorage in Gravesend Bay off Brooklyn. The fleet of smaller boats was divided into small flotillas which were scheduled to pass under Brooklyn Bridge at fifteen minute intervals as a foretaste to New Yorkers of better things to come on the following day.

I overestimated the time it would take to Execution Rock and subsequently *Gipsy Moth* arrived well before our allotted time. We found a convenient anchorage for lunch where it was possible to eat in peace and watch preceding flotillas pass. Eventually the bright red hulls

who had a boat was making their way to the Hudson. Motorboats roared past, sailing yachts plodded along in company; all heading for the carnival. My favourite was a speed enthusiast who performed high-powered wheels and turns around *Gipsy Moth*. The display over, he creamed alongside, slammed the engines into reverse, and unslinging his Instamatic said, 'Smile, fellas.'

The arrangement was that the inshore fleet would be distributed among various ports at the southwest end of the Sound. *Gipsy Moth*, along with *Regina Maris* and *Unicorn*, was invited to the Indian Harbour Yacht Club at Greenwich, Connecticut where the crews were entertained to an elaborate buffet. For us it was the gastronomic highlight of our visit to America. The official party ended quite early, so Minke, Dave and I carried on to a nearby town with recently acquainted friends to dance and loon the night away.

We were slightly apprehensive the next morning

Polonez *sailing down the East River towards the anchorage.*

Christian Radich *being manoeuvred by a tug in New York Harbour.*

of *Kukri* and *Sabre* appeared, so we weighed anchor to join our group. *Norseman*, joining at the same time, dipped her ensign to *Gipsy Moth*, and as we dipped in reply Giles doffed his peaked cap which seemed an appropriate thing to do in the circumstances. At our maximum speed of five knots under power, *Gipsy Moth* was soon left behind by the others. One boat we did overhaul was *Polonez*. Chris, always the purist, had his yacht short-tacking across the East River rather than resort to engine. Perhaps, to give New Yorkers a better preview, all the boats should have sailed rather than used their motors, but the peacock lay dormant in us. Besides, display needs an audience, and while there may well have been spectators surreptitiously peering from office buildings, we couldn't see them.

There was nothing remarkable about the passage until Manhattan's skyline came into view. I've seen dozens of pictures and postcards depicting the Island; not one prepared me for that first sight of it. Surroundings don't often make a great impression on me. Manhattan's uncompromising salute to the architect's audacity had a stark beauty outside my previous experience. An eighteenth century Englishman visiting Scotland described the rugged scenery as 'awful'. Not implying thereby that the scenery was bad, but that it was full of awe. An observation mirroring my reaction to Manhattan.

An ebbing tide carried *Gipsy Moth* to Gravesend. Later, *Polonez* made fast alongside and both yachts swung quietly to *Gipsy Moth*'s anchor. The anchorage was occupied by sailing vessels ranging in size from *Amerigo Vespucci*, a giant dominating the scene, to tiny spectator day boats. *Tovarishch*, *Ticonderoga*, *Leonid Teliga*, the enormous *Club Méditerranée*, recently arrived from the Singlehanded Transatlantic Race, and many

Amerigo Vespucci *at
the Sandy Hook
anchorage (above),
which was shared with such
other vessels as* Club
Méditerranée *(below).*

*Pre-parade
confrontations.*

*Crews manned yards as
the Parade of Sail got
under way.*
Deliverance *nearest the
camera (below).*

Part of the flotilla of replicas of traditional wooden Dutch boats, with crews in costume.

there must have been a secret amendment to the Sailing Instructions. For an hour or two everyone sailed round in circles avoiding collision. Not that there was any intended discourtesy or bad seamanship: helmsmen were merely distracted by the sights. The United States must boast the largest fleet of replica sailing ships in the world, and it was fascinating to avoid an Elizabethan contraption at one turn and the schooner *America* at the next. Traditional Dutch barges adorned with their crews in period costume also contributed to the gaiety and historical confusion. Eventually the square-rigged ships passed at designated twenty-minute intervals and the circling antics in our area stopped as boats jostled for position in their parade order.

A group with a vessel representing each participating nation was first to follow the tall ships. The next squadron in line was made up of large schooners and other comparably sized boats. Then came the nine traditional Dutch barges led by *Eendracht*, Holland's Sail Training Association schooner. Next the biggest of all, our batch, with eighty-seven yachts. Behind us, in meticulous order, came a German flotilla of forty-eight small yachts, especially transported from Germany for the occasion by cargo boat. They were followed by a group of classic sailing yachts from Raritan Bay, New Jersey. And finally came Alain Colas, now abundantly assisted in his *Club Méditerranée*.

In all there were over two hundred vessels, making up as far as I can imagine, the widest range in type and rig ever seen together. The fleet was bolstered further by fifty warships of the International Naval Review which lay to anchor lining the parade route. Yachts passing between them tended to salute by dipping their ensigns or making some similar acknowledgment. It was a measure of the goodwill about that a dhow crew from

others were there. (Op Sail's organizers had waived the S.T.A. rule to include 'character' yachts and other vessels which had not entered any of the races in the Parade of Sail.) Dinghies carrying ships' crews plied between boats on social errands. Ashore, motor cars crawled bumper to bumper, their occupants interested in the assembled fleet rather than making their way home.

The 4th of July dawned without sympathy from the sun. A thin fog enveloped the anchorage, hiding activity on all but the nearer yachts. But activity there was – most had weighed anchor and were under way long before time. Even those that dallied to recheck their manuals for the starting time were swept along by the bustle and presumably assumed, as we did, that with everyone else either under way or getting under way,

Fugil, one of the least known Trucial States, waved as they passed an Israeli gunboat.

To keep the fleet and spectator craft under control a hundred and ninety-six vessels from the Coast Guard Auxiliary were used. They did a magnificent job. When the parade concertinaed, they got it moving. When it spread, they closed it up. Spectator craft breaching the fifty yards clear water on either side of the parade were asked to move away politely once, maybe twice. Then, if they persisted, the Coast Guards closed in with sirens at full blast shouting through loudhailers the inevitable, 'Little boat, get your goddamned ass out of here.' One spectator boat did manage to escape the Coast Guard net to sail along brazenly within the fleet. I admired his pluck, but thought he overacted the nonchalant bit to be totally inconspicuous.

We passed the aircraft carrier U.S.S. *Forrestal* from which President Ford reviewed the sailing fleet. We passed firefighting boats discharging their immense water plumage. And the Statue of Liberty. As participants, our enjoyment was to be there; the spectacle was for those who could see the parade. Confined as we were to a small part of the whole, our entertainment lay with other participants in the immediate vicinity. *G.B. II* sang the usual chorus plus another in their repertoire, 'Happy Birthday America'. (*Master Builder* carried a placard to that effect, so probably deserves composition credits.) *Outlaw* joined the songsters with the first verse of 'Rule Britannia' to each ship in the International Review. Their performance differed slightly from *G.B. II*'s with the introduction of a stylized arm wave set to music. Again *Master Builder* must take credit for the arm wave, having perfected the technique during the 1974 Tall Ships Race.

Generally it was the boats which had joined, or whose

The four U.S. Naval Academy yawls sailing in formation. Rattlesnake is a 71 ft modern replica of a famous eighteenth century American privateer.

America, *a replica of the famous racing schooner, near the Spuyten Duyvil Bridge over the Hudson River, turning point for the Parade.*

The rain squall drenching one of the Baltic ketches, Carola.

crews had joined, in Bermuda and afterwards that were the best performers. They were keen to demonstrate their sail handling ability and man crosstrees; the people who had sailed all the way from Europe seemed content to observe proceedings as spectators within the fleet rather than be obvious contributors to the event.

A highlight in the day for me were the four yawls *Active, Dandy, Flirt* and *Fearless* from the U.S. Naval Academy Sailing Squadron which sailed in perfect formation, line abreast, under spinnakers. To do this under normal circumstances is difficult enough, but the Hudson River on the bicentennial 4th of July seemed suicidal. They made a great impression.

As the parade progressed, the sense of occasion and carnival atmosphere gradually changed on *Gipsy Moth.* A curiosity about New York crept in. Other than Giles and his friends, no-one on board had been there and we were all naturally keen to see the city. Just past Manhattan the wind shifted 180° and soon afterwards a vicious rain and hail storm swept down the Hudson. Ashore, thousands of people ran for shelter and boats in our area suddenly blossomed with crew in blue, yellow and orange, the international variety in oilskin colours. Ahead, the square-rigged ships which had already turned at the George Washington Bridge had their people aloft frantically taking canvas in. The squall passed as quickly as it came. *Christian Radich* made sail, and we dipped into our berth at Pier 92 near West 56th Street. The bloated carcass of a dog floating among other garbage made me reluctant to moor in our allocated spot and we moved back a few yards along the pier away from the rubbish. An adamant piermaster pointed out that a warship from the Review Fleet was destined for the berth at 8 o'clock and we should move by then.

Gipsy Moth's mooring lines were barely secured when we discovered that Molly and Henry Dallas had arrived from Bermuda. We were delighted to see them again, and invited them to join us on board later for the fireworks off Governor's Island, Liberty Island and Ellis Island, below the tip of Manhattan.

Motoring down river to Lower Manhattan that evening, *Gipsy Moth* was well down on her marks with a party of thirteen on board. The fireworks display, as promised, was a suitable finale to America's Bicentennial day. Our comments are surpassed by this official description.

America's most glorious Fourth will be historically celebrated in New York City through the generous gift to the City and America by Macy's New York. Walt Disney Productions' experts, selected to produce the event by the donor, employed their vast resources to choreograph this display, which will bring to the hearts of millions of Americans the true significance of this occasion.

The production will begin precisely at 9.00 p.m. on the evening of July 4, 1976 with the chiming of the hour and sounding of a Westminster peel.

The Fireworks Show represents the largest peacetime installation of guns and mortars for entertainment purposes ever assembled in the United States.

Disney designed shells appearing in the display have been made expressly for this production in Japan, Taiwan, Korea, France, Brazil, Canada and the United States. They range in size from three to twelve inches in circumference and ignite in the sky from 400 to 1,500 feet. Each of the over 3,000 shells is electronically cued to fire and burst at a precise moment in the patriotic musical production that will accompany the display.

Adding to the pageantry will be thirteen sky searchlights, one for each original colony, forming a crown above the Statue of Liberty. A particularly dramatic moment will occur prior to the fireworks as a 200 gun salute is sounded from guns aboard ships anchored round the Harbor. The broadcast portion of the show will be aired on radio, television and public address systems throughout the area.

The computer-like cueing system, programming of each shell, radio broadcast and musical accompaniment to visual aerial pyrotechnics, make this production, indeed, a work of animated art in fireworks.

Impressions of New York remain now as they occurred at the time. A blurred interlude into which we packed too much for anything to make sense. Sightseeing with Sue, Giles and Arthur as our expert guides to the city: Central Park, the Lincoln Center, Greenwich Village, Chinatown, the World Trade Center. Gratitude for Sue's apartment as an air-conditioned oasis in the humidity. A tickertape parade along Broadway. Attempting to unravel the subway system. Jets of steam from the manhole covers. Molten tarmac. People, parties, sightseers, boats – it was bewildering.

Returning from the tickertape parade, I looked down from the quay at *Gipsy Moth* lying alongside *Juan Sebastian de Elcano*, a midget besides the Spanish barquentine. Something in her lines, or perhaps knowing the purpose for which she was built, made me despair to see her tied up like that. It was sad, and I longed to be at sea again. Caroline phoned Tim Peirce to accept his invitation to Westport and we sailed the following morning.

Gipsy Moth retraced her route through the East River towards the Sound. At Hell Gate an adverse tide sluicing through the Narrows virtually halted progress. A Coast Guard launch, seeing our predicament, passed a line to tow us clear. We re-entered Long Island Sound without further delay to arrive at Westport, Connecticut ahead of schedule. Timing was a bit critical since the approach channel had a maximum depth of eight feet or

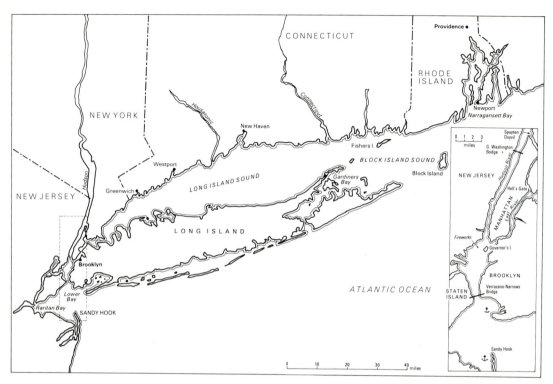

The largest vessels which took part in the Parade of Sail were routed to New York outside Long Island; Gipsy Moth and most of the other yachts sailed from Newport, Rhode Island via Long Island Sound and the East River into New York Harbour and their assigned anchorages in Lower Bay, between Staten Island, the New Jersey shore and Brooklyn.

The tickertape parade for the Tall Ships Race crews, between the walls of lower Manhattan (right).

Official reception at City Hall in New York on July 5th. In the foreground are the skippers of the Race and Op Sail vessels.

The all-female crew of Sir Winston Churchill on the leg from Bermuda to New York was sponsored by Royal Insurance. The girls were issued with several uniform changes ; here, straw boater and Trafalgar collar for going-ashore kit (right).

so at high water, only inches more than our draft. We met our pilot David Rogers, a Naval Reserve commander and friend of Tim's, at the outer buoy. He transferred on board from his launch and piloted *Gipsy Moth* to a nearby marina where fuel and water were available and where we could wait the tide.

When the tide had risen sufficiently, we left for Westport's Saugatuch Yacht Club to receive a tremendous reception and even the key to Westport. Afterwards Tim invited us to a barbecue party at his home.

We set out again the next morning. *Gipsy Moth* was expected for the Boston Parade of Sail on July 10, which left only forty-eight hours to get there. That night, after an uneventful day's sail, we chose a quiet mooring, so remote I've forgotten where. It provided what we needed most of all, a full and uninterrupted night's sleep – the first and last we were to have in America.

A nonsense came the following evening at the entrance to the Cape Cod Canal. Visibility, which had deteriorated through the afternoon from poor to rotten, suddenly became impossible. It was not on to anchor in the canal, but I had noticed an indentation on the chart which could amount to a small harbour. We headed in roughly the right direction and sure enough sensed, rather than found, a little resting spot for tugs. Then the game began. In the first attempt to come alongside, the bow paid off and a tugman came on deck to take our lines. The bow still paid off in a second approach, after allowances for current. I tried again and still a nause. Thoroughly annoyed, I attempted portside too. This time the stern paid but we had a bow line on, which, as the stern continued to slip away, we let go. On the fifth attempt, the tugman leant casually over his bulwark and said, 'Give it the gun next time round fella. You're on a whirlpool there.' With this fortuitous advice we were

Canadian sail training ship Pathfinder

able to secure alongside.

In waiting for the fog to clear we missed the tide through the Cape Cod Canal and subsequently the Boston parade.

The mooring pontoon at Boston recaptured to some extent the air of preparation prevalent in Tenerife. It differed in that the boats were now getting ready for an Atlantic crossing after an event rather than sailing to one. Lying alongside *Stortebeker*, we recalled the earlier anticipations. Both boats were now completely stripped out for a thorough scrub and checkover, but *Stortebeker*'s people were to fly home, to be replaced by an unknown crew. A similar situation occurred with many crews we had come to know. Our personal loss was Roger Bonnett, who departed for England sooner than expected, lured by Bath Festival and the song of his Siren who lives there. *Gipsy Moth*, back to her original crew of seven, seemed empty without him. Perhaps the greatest melancholy came when *Dar Pormoza* slipped her moorings, taking not only her crew but friends from

Polonez back to Poland. (Chris Baranowski stayed in America with *Polonez* to be joined by his wife and family for an extended cruise.) I'm sure that people on other boats felt similarly about seeing their friends leave. For me, *Dar Pormoza* particularly symbolized in size as well as in her crew what the S.T.A. Tall Ships Races meant: the opportunity to meet other nations pursuing their own way of life with a mutual goal. My Utopian dream is that one day mankind will outgrow the competitive urge. In the meanwhile, if friendly competition achieves the international melting pot, I'm for it – with a will to win.

On the bright side, John Hamilton joined *Great Britain II* as skipper and Adrian Bomback remained on board as navigator. While John was able to sing along with the rest of them, he took leg-pulling on that account in good part. Adrian's wry sense of humour had flourished over a hamburger in Newport and had seldom failed since then. *Gladan*'s original crew remained, and for additional interest in the coming crossing we set up a race within a race between *Gipsy Moth* and *Gladan*. Both crews agreed that the two boats were evenly matched on handicap; providing each was sailed flat out, the outcome would depend on weather conditions. Sten Gattberg, *Gladan*'s captain, reckoned his schooner's only real bête noire was coping with short seas in lightish winds. I had no complaints about *Gipsy Moth* other than her being slightly undercanvassed in light airs to windward. Our main problem would be overcoming the handicap downwind in force 4 or above, where *Gladan* excelled. The odds were even, and Liptons capped the idea by offering a sovereign to the winner.

A diversion from the pre-departure rigmarole came when the Queen and the Duke of Edinburgh arrived in

Boston. Crews from the United Kingdom lined the procession route. Later, as the Queen and Duke returned to *Britannia* after a visit to U.S.S. *Constitution* (which incidentally caused the Royal Navy considerable aggravation in the 1812 Anglo-American war), the skippers from British yachts were presented. *Britannia* sailed for Canada that evening.

The American episode in the Tall Ships event was over. In Boston, the participants met the same hospitality that featured throughout the United States visit. Parties were too frequent to mention individually, but these, not unlike sail changes, fitted into the good, bad or indifferent category (though I'm no judge, preferring to avoid organized celebrations for small and impromptu gatherings). The various Op Sail committees and the American Sail Training Association did everything they could, and more, to assure their guests' welcome and for the general success of the event. In England we were often told that when we arrived in America our feet wouldn't touch the ground. This was a metaphorical understatement. One day I hope to return firmly weighed down with soil in my boots.

H.R.H. the Queen and the Duke of Edinburgh meet the skippers of the British entries at Boston. From left: Esmond Friend of Cameo of Looe, *Peter Hambly, Bruce Thorogood and Fred Dovaston from* Master Builder, *Brian Watson of* Lindø, *an unidentified person, Robert Fewtrell of* Outlaw, *Capt. C. P. R. Collis of* Winston Churchill *(in whites). James Myatt from* Great Britain II *is in the right foreground next to the Duke. The Royal Yacht* Britannia *is behind them, and the spars of U.S.S.* Constitution *in the background.*

Leg 4 – Boston to Plymouth, England

Of the original fleet twenty-one vessels started at Boston for the transatlantic race back to Plymouth, England. Others had sailed north to the Olympic Games in Canada; some, from the Mediterranean contingent, sailed back to their countries direct; others remained in the U.S.A. This final race was actually only a minor event organized by the S.T.A. as a kindness to provide competitive conditions for those who wished to race on their way home. As an out-and-out race it may have been a disappointment to some, but as an exercise in friendly rivalry it was probably the best of the entire series.

Gladan, which had taken on the job of communications vessel, did much to foster this. Talking with her radio operator had all the informality of speaking to a fellow competitor rather than to a telephone answering service. This is not intended as a criticism of the earlier vessels responsible for communications: they had their time cut out, coping with a much larger fleet. How *Gladan* really influenced general cordiality was by re-transmitting the weathe forecasts obtained with her transatlantic receivers. And naturally Swedish pronunciation brought colourful variety compared to the orthodox British radio voice.

In Boston, listening around, I gathered that most competitors intended to sail due east leaving the Gulf Stream some hundred miles to the south. According to the Pilot Charts, this course gave marginally more wind but an adverse current. Dave and I discussed the alternatives and for several reasons decided to follow the Gulf Stream as far as the southeastern end of Newfoundland and then branch north on the great circle route. In a minor way our choice was an emotional decision. We couldn't resist an attempt at using the Gulf Stream's advantageous currents after the adverse tricks it had played in the third leg. Emotion aside, it seemed from the charts that unless we were totally becalmed the current advantage outweighed the more direct and windier northern course. Fog was also a consideration. Across the Newfoundland Banks it was an above

The final start at Boston attracted as large a spectator fleet as anywhere, here seen from the British Army yacht Kukri.

Garfunkle plotting courses in hopes of using the Gulf Stream.

average probability while the Gulf Stream appeared relatively free of it.

After staying longer at the fueling berth than planned, we started well behind everyone else (having met the spectator fleet on their way home). Fortunately we found the conditions that produce magic from *Gipsy Moth V*. With light winds, no sea, and sailing on a point somewhere slightly above a reach, she performs exceptionally well. It was her peculiar characteristic that given those conditions she could overhaul the best of them and almost keep pace with *G.B. II*.

Our course inclining more towards the south took us away from the main bunch and they were lost to sight before sunset. That night the watches were kept busy avoiding fishing boats which abound in the area, and some cargo ships. Visibility, poor as usual, kept lookouts peering into the murk. Engine noises were usually the first warning we had that a vessel was in the vicinity. Some boats we saw, but mainly they passed close by as a mere noise in the fog. Psychologically the visibility improved at daybreak, although in reality it was probably just as bad only less claustrophobic.

The morning radio schedule confirmed general tactics. Everyone other than *Gipsy Moth* and *Urania* had chosen to sail due east rather than take the dip south. *Urania* had made a definite leg south as opposed to our gradual inclination in that direction. This positive move, judging by her position further to the east, had evidently paid off.

The first radio schedule also illustrated what creatures of habit we had become and how easily we slipped back into sea routines. Ten minutes before call-up time I turned the battery power supply on, sharpened a pencil and went to the loo. Coming back to the chart table, Clive asked, as he invariably did, 'Have you switched the ovens on?' 'Ovens' was marked on our transmitter by the manufacturer. Quite what they were, I didn't know, but during the post-installation briefing, the expert explained that they had to be switched on ten minutes before broadcasting. Clive's query came from a time early in the cruise when I sat twiddling dials in frenzied blasphemy trying to tune the set only to find that the ovens were off.

While I listened and logged reported positions, Garfunkel sitting at the main saloon table plotted them on graph paper marked in appropriate latitude and longitude. At a glance he could tell the progress of every boat in the fleet. Whoever was on cook day duty made coffee, and everyone other than the helmsman hung about either listening near the chart table or watching over Garfunkel's shoulder.

Supper and the radio schedule were the main events of the day. Sailing the boat was as exhilarating as ever but physical responses had become automatic. The girls vied with the men to change sails – everyone wanted the exercise. Even setting up the unwieldy running booms, which called for minor acrobatics at the mast, became a piffling task to the girls. Minke excelled at the acrobatics, and Rosie led sheets and attached guys, topping lifts and halliards with unassumed confidence. During the sail from St George's to Hamilton in Bermuda, the male faction had quietly decided to leave the manual bit entirely to the girls. It backfired. They tacked around the reefs all afternoon piloted by Steve Dallas and brought Gipsy Moth into Hamilton unaware of our absence from the winches.

Dave had throughout the voyage taught anyone who was interested how to navigate. By the time we arrived back in Plymouth I think everyone on board could work and plot a sun sight. Dave took special care with Minke's tuition as a first step in their ultimate dream to cruise around the world.

The race to Plymouth had two hiccups outside my previous experience. One an unusual phenomenon; the second, whales. On our third night out, at the midnight watch change, Gipsy Moth after slipping along easily on a broad reach suddenly sailed into a completely windless area. Booms, previously held forward by the wind in their sails, swung listlessly amidships hanging from their limp canvas. Still darkness encroached, emphasizing our isolation. From starboard came the sound of distant breakers approaching slowly. In my days at sea I have seen enough of the inexplicable to shut up about it, reasoning that there's no point in losing personal credibility by describing the incredible. On this occasion my imagination recalling former occurrences groped for an explanation. Nothing came to mind. Dave, careering down the companion hatch for the Aldis lamp, murmured 'whales'. At least a thought to cling to, but at its extreme range the lamp beam only revealed disturbed sea which could have been caused by anything. The regularity of the noise we heard made me doubt that it came from a playful school of whales thrashing about.

Worldwide, the annual loss of yachts without trace is not inconsiderable. The average motorist, disregarding the 'it can never happen to me' mental buffer, must be aware that, however unlikely, the possibility of death in a road accident exists. In sailing, although the odds are reduced the same possibility exists. The subtle difference, to me, lies in the 'without trace' condition. I can reconcile myself to the possibility of a mishap, but what I find an intolerable burden on my friends is the void left for the imaginations by this idea. I feel obliged, in indulging a selfish pastime, at least to have the courtesy to leave a definite epitaph.

As the breakers came nearer to *Gipsy Moth* I found myself reiterating those thoughts. And assuming that everyone on board felt similarly, said, in macabre humour, 'Lousy way to become a statistic.' Judging from Rosemary's face, that was quite the wrong thing to say (her diary confirmed this). The possibility of danger merely by the sound of breakers hadn't occurred to her. On the other hand, I recognized in Dave's face, drawn with the deliberate non-commitment he saved for such occasions, the anxiety I felt.

The breaking waves crept on, eventually washing against *Gipsy Moth*'s side. Dave, armed with the Aldis, again scanned the water beyond the initial turbulence seeking a maelstrom. Nothing. A few yards of broken water, then the sea appeared perfectly normal again. We searched for an explanation. The chart showed a constant depth – not even an unnatural contour. The only thing we could think might have caused it was that the area had temporarily become a meeting point for the opposing Labrador and Gulf Stream currents. Gulf Stream meanders are notorious, and one of these may have nudged sharply against the contrary Labrador Current, giving the sea conditions we saw.

Shortly after this trauma the wind got up, bringing *Gipsy Moth* back to life. She tore along the easting for two days with shrouds and backstays strumming her passage. Man and boat became as one again, the last cobwebs of land forgotten. Somewhere in that mad dash we raced past *Urania* leaving her a half mile or so to port. If paradise could promise me *Gipsy Moth* reaching in a force 5 or 6, I'd be tempted to take holy orders. But, alas, pleasure is finite on earth. The point where we intended to head up on the great circle route was bedevilled by calm and *Gipsy Moth* decelerated into it.

Around about this time a metamorphosis happened in our general attitude. The race itself ceased to matter; neither were we particularly concerned by the competitors who, while we lay becalmed, ate into the distance *Gipsy Moth* had made. What we were concerned about was enjoying the sail. This was the last opportunity to indulge our freedom. England lay ahead. It was a return to certainty rather than the possibility of discovering our expectations: we had become accustomed to constant change in the past months. While everyone wanted to get back to England, no one wanted to give up the dream. Tensions, contradictions and minor irritation crept into our daily lives, inexplicable except in retrospect.

In the calm *Gipsy Moth* slowed down to a snail's pace. The log flickered between $\frac{1}{2}$ and $1\frac{1}{2}$ knots, at such minimal speed avoiding even the noise made by slatting sails. By noon, the sun had regained something of its tropical strength despite the latest ice reports positioning icebergs less than 200 miles away. Hawkeye Clive, ever vigilant, spotted what he thought was an abandoned yacht. We altered course for a closer look, and it did seem for a while that the yacht was steered supernaturally. Just as I was beginning to unleash my imagination on the crew's plight, someone popped up from a lying position in the cockpit. He saw *Gipsy Moth* barely fifty yards away and called down the companion hatch; three more figures bobbed up in quick succession. We chatted about the weather, exchanged good wishes and resumed course. The sloop *Bobsy III* was one of the forty-eight yachts from West Germany transported to America by cargo boat for the New York Parade of Sail. They had been becalmed for two days.

A southerly wind set in an hour after midnight, ending a day when we lost ground to the entire fleet.

Every morning, the Duty Galley Rat of Kukri *made bread— some with more success than others.*

The sloping loaf.

Germania and *G.B. II* increased their marginal lead, *Sabre* and *Kukri* overhauled us, the remainder caught up. *Gladan*, leading on handicap from the first day out, improved her time. Our will to win had disappeared but the mechanisms to do so, in crew and boat, were still completely functional. With the first sign of a reaching wind the big balloon topsail shot up its track, followed minutes later by the running gear. As the downwind canvas went up *Gipsy Moth* gained speed, each sail increasing her momentum until, with the final adjustments to mizzen and balloon topsail sheets, she danced along at her maximum speed.

At this juncture we were lying further south than the others, giving us slightly more flexibility in course over the northern boats. *Germania* had from the start chosen to sail close to Newfoundland and her speed from day to day increased, outstripping even *G.B. II*. We found it difficult to assess whether the boats which had had new crews join in Boston were improving their performance or whether they were getting better wind. In the past days we had kept pace with *Germania*, *G.B. II*, *Kukri* and *Sabre*, mainly because their crews were comparatively inexperienced. But after a week at sea it was reasonable to assume that they had recovered from sea-sickness and were becoming useful on deck. Relative positions remained more or less the same in the next two days until once again we sailed into lighter winds.

By this time a wireless repartee between *Gipsy Moth* and *G.B. II* was in full swing, and we normally swapped abuse and weather information after *Gladan*'s evening broadcast. On that particular evening, having sailed into light winds, I was keen to know how *G.B. II*, about a hundred miles ahead, was getting on and asked John over the radio. After some 'ums' and 'aahs' and mocking enquiries about the frankfurters he had given us in

Boston (*G.B. II*'s crew loathed them), he said, 'Oh, we're sailing reasonably on a starboard tack steering 045° but it smells a lot.' This indirectly gave me all the information I had asked for without disclosing it to *Germania*, their rival for the finishing line. From past conversations ashore with John and Adrian I knew that *G.B. II*'s bilges ponged when she was closehauled in rough seas. So in other words she was in an easterly wind of at least force 5 or 6. Back in England, John confirmed this and enlarged on it. Apparently while we were talking *G.B. II* was pressed well over. The mate had his watch tramping about on deck for a headsail change and John clung to the chart table with one hand while he worked the microphone presser switch and tried to muffle revealing extraneous noises from deck with the other.

At our end there was also a major commotion from on deck. Sitting by the radio, I could see everyone standing

aft and looking astern, obviously agitated. Garfunkel dived below to grab the binoculars hanging near my shoulder, and said 'There's a bloody great school of whales coming up astern.' I quickly ended the conversation and almost turned the radio off, then thought better of it and tuned to the 2182 instead. By the time I joined the others, speculation on what species the whales were had reached a fairly excited level. Garfunkel, equipped with binoculars, gave a running commentary, surmising that they were too small to be sperm and too large to be dolphins. They came on, churning the sea, and eventually he narrowed the species to two possibilities: they were either killer or pilot whales. 'Killers'. That caused an eruption. Were they the ones that sank the Robinsons' yacht, nearly sank Bill King, and had those other people adrift in a rubber raft for 119 days? And still they came on directly in the wake. At forty yards off we were still undecided about their type, none of us having seen a whale before. We estimated that there were thirty altogether, ranging in size from the largest at thirty feet to young calves ten feet long swimming in company with their mothers. They kept that distance for a while and then came on again to play a few feet at either side and astern. Garfunkel had by this time definitely decreed that they were pilot whales. Even so, I fervently hoped that the virile bucks diving underneath our hull would not mistake *Gipsy Moth* for an eligible cow.

Later that evening we got similar weather conditions to *Great Britain II*, although my estimate of wind strength made from the earlier radio chat was a few knots too low. It was a novelty for us to reef the mizzen. In three months underway we had seldom sailed to windward, and only once in wind strengths that called for a reef. This may be slightly misleading to those who

sail a straightforward Bermudan sloop where reefing becomes as commonplace as breakfast or lunch. On *Gipsy Moth V* the unusual sail plan gave tremendous versatility and normally it was more advantageous in time, performance and ease to drop a staysail rather than mess about reefing the mizzen. Incidentally, it was the only sail on board where the designer had made provision for reef points; nor was there roller reefing: sails were intended to be lowered instead of reduced in area.

Something that has deterred me in recent years from reading voyage accounts in yachting magazines is a fear that the author might describe an exhilarating thrash to windward. While I understand the enthusiasm and still enjoy some measure of it, providing there's a hot shower available at the end of the day, there's now nothing in yachts I loathe more than sailing to windward for days on end in big seas. Everything from peeing to cooking becomes a major task. The discomfort is an insidious process which invariably begins with damp, or even worse, water creeping inside oilskins. No matter how tight and well constructed the boat, water either from the sea or from condensation eventually finds its way below for the final misery – a wet sleeping bag. Slamming gives me another neurosis about windward work. I appreciate how technology has improved strength in yacht construction and rigging, but I cannot watch chainplates, shrouds and stays under those stresses without wondering how long they will hold. This phobia for slamming also extends to the purely physical, reasoning that my metabolism can never adapt to the jarring crack as the yacht stops and shudders in its track. But the metabolism does adapt; it takes on average three days to grow accustomed to life at an angle (based on observations made on various O.Y.C.

cruises). Purgatory lies in seeing those initial days through.

I think the changed weather did in fact hasten one or two rigging problems on board. The port masthead jib halliard block sheared at its swivel one evening, causing us to wonder at first who had eased the sheet. Having partially dropped, the jib sounded as if it was inadequately sheeted rather than undone. After some ineffectual winching, someone went forward to investigate and shouted back the news. The duty watch handed the jib, attached the starboard halliard and rehoisted it. Dave then got his climbing boots on and attached a new masthead block.

The other rigging trouble came after several days' hard going to windward when the port forestay's rigging screw sheared. Fortunately Sir Francis had provided for such a contingency, and we were able to rig the spare with nothing worse than a thorough dousing on the foredeck.

Shortly after that was sorted out, a fault cropped up in the paraffin stove's pressure pump, causing some concern for our diet. Clive, who during the voyage had become an expert stove engineer, quickly had the whole caboodle dissembled only to be faced with what seemed an insurmountable problem. The pump's outer casing was welded at the join making the inner washer, which by the sound of it had worn out, inaccessible. Forcing the join with vice and Mole Grips seemed an obvious solution, but this might have caused distortion in the cylinder. As we reconciled ourselves to thoughts of uncooked vegetables and cold tinned concoctions, Dave remembered the tiny emergency Primus he had brought along. He and Clive set about stoking it (no mean feat at our heeling angle) and after a flare-up or two got it working well enough to melt the weld on the stove pump. After that it was simple. I fashioned a new washer from Caroline's leather belt and Clive reassembled the pump and soldered the join. We celebrated with a cup of coffee.

Those clinging-on days seemed an interminable episode where life on board declined into a tedious existence. The ladies, Caroline and Rosemary, kept smiling and brought occasional perspective to the general gloom. But the gloom didn't last. When the wind eventually died everyone emerged from their insularity to resume as before; a cog in the common lot.

With only 500 miles to go, and given good reaching conditions, we were within two days' sail of Plymouth. But fate had other ideas. The wind wafting at luxurious strength remained easterly. In that last 500 miles the overall race pattern changed completely. *Gladan*, days ahead of everyone on handicap, suddenly found her *bête noire* sailing conditions. The four lead boats, *Kukri*, *Sabre*, *G.B. II* and *Germania*, managed to hold a private windstream and finished while the remaining vessels were stuck in a high pressure area. In the heavy going to windward we had lost surprisingly little ground to the sloops in Division II, but in light airs *Gipsy Moth* was slightly undercanvassed on the wind and of course could not point as high as the sloops. When we moved onto the 'Approaches to the English Channel' chart we crossed tacks with *Outlaw* and saw *Stortebeker* in the distance. *Carillion of Wight, Glénan* and *Walross III* were all within a thirty mile radius of our position. *Master Builder* carried an insurmountable T.C.F. no matter what the weather.

After six days of tacks and counter tacks Bishop Rock off the Scilly Isles appeared through the heat haze. I put a link call through Lands End Radio to Julian Hill and my wife Jen. Julian bubbled with enthusiasm when he heard our position, and although I explained that we were totally becalmed he maintained a sublime confidence that we would arrive at Plymouth in a matter of hours. And sure enough, soon after I turned the radio off a faint southeasterly breeze filled the sails. *Gipsy Moth* trickled along and gradually picked up speed throughout the day. By sunset she was tearing past the Lizard giving a final demonstration of her magic.

We crossed the finishing line off the Eddystone light at 4.30 in the morning. *Gipsy Moth* had sailed nearly 10,000 miles in the 97 days she was away from Plymouth. In her class, she won the last race on handicap. *Gladan* came second, only half an hour behind on handicap.

In Millbay Dock, Giles Chichester and Alf Boxer from Liptons welcomed us with a champagne breakfast and an enormous lunch. It was odd to be back. Realized dreams are mere experiences, but it does make room for new ones.

The Tea-Clipper's Lament

I've been a tea-clipper since many's the year:
It's a trade that is passing, you see,
For the youngsters today just can't understand
You won't get hairs on your chest if you don't drink
   your tea.

It was in the summer of '76
By 'eck I remember it well – Oh, arrr!
When *Gipsy Moth V* was due to arrive
At Bermuda – the story I'll tell:

She was a trim craft rigged all fore and aft
But the Jasmine was running low,
We'd a hole in the teapot, the spout was all bent
And the wind it threatened to blow.

Hambly was pacing the quarterdeck
A worried man by now,
Clad only in Y-fronts and a tatty string vest
A cold teabag clamped to his brow.

The Jasmine was low – what a terrible blow
And the Samovar wasn't much better,
So what was to do to prevent the whole crew
From writing Liptons a letter?

He thought of Ceylon with a gleam in his eye
For the taste set his ardour a-quiver,
'But,' he thought with a wince, 'it's only two days
   since
It played bloody 'ell with me liver!'

So that was no good: 'What of China?' he thought,
And his mind began to race
A bouquet soigné and a soupçon of scent –
He dreamily stroked at his face.

He laughed and lifted his wintery head
Heavy with the burden of years,
As his thoughts flew back to his mates on the shore
His old eyes misted with tears.

There was Julian of course, a swaggering young blade
With a devilish glint in his eye.
Why he's sunk many a pint of steaming tea
And oft drunk the teapot dry!

And big John D., the bold buccaneer
Who ploughed the Spanish main
Until someone slipped him a coffee bean:
He was never heard of again.

And Alf the Great, a jolly jack tar
With many a quip and a jest.
Why he knew his teas (and his onions too)
And brimmed over with life and with zest.

But Hambly's dreams are shattered soon
For a din breaks out below:
The tea strainer's snapped clean in half,
And the crew cries out 'Oh blow!'

Old Hambly's mind is racing now:
'What can save the day?
Teabags? Camomile? Darjeeling?
Or maybe a spot of Early Grey?'

A sudden thought comes to his mind,
His watch says half-past six.
He runs, and bellows to his crews
'I'll see you through this fix!

Just hang on 'til the sun's well up
for now it's plain to see
That what we need is Lipton's
Special English Breakfast Tea!'

Epilogue and Chorus
Oh I'm a Tea Clipper. I spend my time
A-clipping tea at sea
Clip, clip, clip, the clippers go
That's the life for me!
When this old clipper's dead and gone
Just pickle me in tea
Preserve my smile with Camomile
And put me out to sea.
And when I get to heaven above
And the Big Tea Maker speaks to me
We'll chat as we savour the delicate flavour
Of Lipton's Special Tea.

Roger wrote and then recorded this poem (with sound effects from the crew) as a gift for Julian Hill at Liptons. The tape was posted to him from Tenerife.

The Great Clipper Race

I thought this extract from *The Bird of Dawning* appropriate since it's the best fictional account I have read of sailing ships racing. Sir Francis Chichester also used it in his anthology *Along the Clipper Way*.

On the second day, the wester, which had been blowing steadily, increased in strength and blew a full true gale, with abundant rain keeping down the sea. They ran before this, day after day, in exultation, striding over an expanse of two thousand miles across. Presently, it became blind going, so that they went by log and a guess; yet still the wind increased, till Mr Fairford looked grave and old Kemble shook his head. Mr Fairford coming up to Cruiser as the night closed in suggested that if anything were coming in, it would be handled more easily in daylight. Cruiser had not been below for more than twenty minutes at a time for a week. He had slept, if at all, in a hammock slung under the weather mizzen pin-rail; the exultation of the wind and the going had entered into him; he shook the rain from his face and grinned back at Fairford.

'Take anything in,' he said. 'I was just thinking if we couldn't set a royal.'

Fairford was too old a sailor to say anything; he looked at the royal mast, and looked to windward, and looked at Cruiser.

Fairford said nothing more about shortening sail. He made one more suggestion: 'I suppose you wouldn't care for a cast of the lead, sir, about midnight tonight? We should be about on soundings, wouldn't we?'

'We're all right,' Cruiser said. 'Why, Mister, you couldn't have the heart to stop her, could you?'

'It's a good slant, sir,' Fairford said. 'But blind going's bad going, if you ask me.'

'She's all right, Mister.'

'Very good, Captain Trewsbury.' Fairford walked to the break of the poop. Efans, the sea-lawyer, was talking to Stratton. 'These poys, look you, they wass not prudent men: they take the sticks clean out of her, as sure as Cot's my uncle.'

All night long she drove before the thrust of the wester, in a succession of staggering and surging leaps that sent the crests of the waves flying white before her. At midnight she was running twelve, at two, thirteen, and at the changing of the watch fourteen knots. Though she had ever steered easily, she was now more than one man's task: the lee wheel was manned, and kept busy.

At five in the morning Cruiser turned out after an hour of uneasy sleep in his hammock to find the ship roaring on up Channel in the breaking darkness, a high grey Channel sea running under a wild heaven, and the teeth of the waves gleaming out from the grey. He lurched to the mate, who was forward, putting an extra tackle on the fore-tack. When the tack was home, he asked:

'Have you picked up any light, Mister?'

'No, sir, all blind as you see.'

'Well, we must be there or thereabouts.'

'Yes, sir. It's been a good slant.'

'Get a hand aloft when it lightens a bit; he may be able to see the land.'

'Very good, Captain Trewsbury.' The mate hesitated for a moment, then said:

'If you please, sir, we're doing more than fourteen, and we haven't had a sight for four days. We're well into the Channel: and thick as it is we may be on top of anything before we see it.'

'No: keep her going,' Cruiser said. 'Our luck's in. We'll not throw it away.'

'Very good, Captain Trewsbury.'

The ship was running on, with the same desperate haste, an hour later when Trewsbury returned. It was now in the wilderness of an angry morning, with a low, hurrying heaven and leaping sea, that showed green under the grey, and rose and slipped away with a roar. The ship was careering with an aching straining crying from every inch of her, aloft and below. Her shrouds strained and whined and sang, the wind boomed in her sail, the sheet blocks beat, the chain of their pendants whacked the masts. All the mighty weight of ship and cargo heaved itself aloft, and surged and descended and swayed, smashing the seas white, boring into and up and out of the hills and the hollows of the water, and singing as she did it, and making all hands, as they toiled, to sing.

'Run, you bright bird,' Trewsbury said, 'that's what you were born to.'

There was no chance of a sight with that low heaven: the man aloft could see nothing: all hands were on deck getting the anchors over. There came a sudden cry from them of 'Steamer, dead ahead.'

She must have seen them on the instant, and ported on the instant, enough to clear. Cruiser saw her as it were climbing slowly and perilously to port for twenty seconds: then as he leaped for the signals flags to ask, 'Where are we?' she was surging past close alongside, a little grey coastal tramp, with a high bridge over her central structure, butting hard into it with a stay foresail dark with wet to steady her, and her muzzle white to the eyes. As she had just fired, a stream of black smoke blew away and down from her, with sudden sparks in it, as Cruiser thought. Cruiser saw two figures in yellow oilskins staring at them from behind the dodger. He knew well with what admiration and delight those sailors stared. Then the little coaster's stern hove up in a smother, as her head dipped to it, and she was past and away, with one man behind the dodger waving a hand. The reek of her smoke struck Cruiser's nostrils; then she was gone from them her name unknown.

The mate was at Cruiser's side.

'That shows you how we're in the fairway, sir,' he said. 'We may be on top of something at any minute. We've only a minute to clear anything, in this.'

'I know it.'

'Yes, sir.'

'Did you ever hear of a China clipper throwing away a fair wind in soundings?'

'No, sir.'

'Did you ever hear of a China clipper being sunk in the Channel when running?'

'No, Captain Trewsbury, and I don't want to be the first.'

'Well, I do want to be the first, Mister, and I mean to be it, the first to London Docks, if you understand. And to get there, I have to use whatever chance throws in my way. It's going to break, presently.'

There came a hail from the main crosstrees, where the lookout had a speaking trumpet. 'Ship on starboard bow.' They turned to look at her, and Cruiser who was ready now ran up the signal flags of, 'What is my position?'

As the flags blew out clear the ship hove up alongside. she was a big full-rigged ship, painted black, and very loftily rigged with skysail yards on all three masts. She was now under her fore and main lower topsails and fore topmast staysail, beating her way down Channel. She was streaming with glittering water. At each 'scend the sea ran white along her rail, which bowed to it and lipped it in. Then, out of the pause, the bowed fabric seemed to dive forward, though with difficulty. Cruiser saw the watch gathered on the poop, all staring; even the man at the wheel was staring. The ship beat past them on a lurching leap, her maindeck full and spouting, no one answering the signal, not even acknowledging it.

'There's discourtesy,' the mate said. 'She wouldn't even dip her colours.'

'She never saw our signal,' Cruiser said. 'She's an outward-bounder, with everything on top and nothing to hand. Besides she was watching us.'

'We must be well worth the watching, sir,' the mate said, moving away. To himself, as he moved, he added, 'and I hope all who meet us will watch out for us.'

It grew lighter in the sky, but no lighter to landward, they were running in a blind and moving seascape not a thousand yards across, all cloud and water, both mad. The ship strode into it, and streaked her way across it, smashing on to the greyness a track of a paleness and a greenness of many million bubbles, over which the petrels scuttered.

Where they were Cruiser did not know, and did not much care. The exultation that was so movingly in the ship was in himself. They were getting up Channel with a marvellous slant, and who could tell that they were not leading the fleet. It would clear up presently, and they would see where they were, or pass something that would tell them.

'Forward there,' he called. 'Up there two of you, and get a good burton on the foreyard. Lively now, I'm going to give her a stunsail.'

'Burton on the foreyard: ay, ay, sir.'

He turned to the helmsmen. Coates, who had the weather spokes, was enjoying it; he loved to see a ship driven; but Bauer at the lee wheel was scared.

'How is she, Coates?' he asked.

'She's begun to be a bit kittenish,' Coates said, 'but nothing to hurt, sir.'

'You're keeping a good course. You can steer, Coates.'

'Yes, sir. And she can kick, I tell you.'

'Keep your eyes forward, Bauer,' Cruiser said. 'There's nothing for you to look at behind you.'

There was, though. There was a toppling, toppling running array of heaping water ever slipping over at the top.

'If you let her broach to, Bauer,' he said, 'you'll be the first man drowned and the last man God will forgive and that's what you'll get by it.'

Bauer smiled a sickly smile, and licked his dry lips and said: 'Yes, sir.'

'All ready the burton, forward?'

'All ready, sir.'

'Bowse it well taut.' He went forward to see to the setting of the sail.

As the courses of the *Bird of Dawning* were very deep as well as square, the lower studding sail was a great sail, needing much care in the setting, in such a wind as was blowing. The boom was run forward and guyed. All hands mustered to the job. They well knew that if it were not done smartly, the sail would go. A wild sea spread from under their feet into the hurrying cloud; but those there felt, from the push of the rain that came down upon them, that the greyness was about to go. The rain that had streamed from all things relented suddenly and died into a pattering.

'Let her go,' Cruiser called. The tackles skirled as the men went away with them; he paid out the tripping line as they ran. The boom dipped under as it went and the great sail darkened with the wet half up it. As the stops came adrift, the sail lifted and strove to flog itself clear, but the checks of the gear came on to it and stayed it. One instant before it had been a bulge of canvas, flapping at folds where the wind could catch it, now it was a straining curve of sail, held by check and countercheck, leaning like a wing to the ship over all that hurry of leaping sea. She put down her foot, and the foot of the sail stooped into it, as a gull stoops upon the wing. She rose, with the water dripping from the scoop, and again plunged and arose shaking.

'That's got her where she lives,' Clutterbucke said. 'That's made her lift her feet.'

'Just as well she's got that burton on her yardarm.'

The effect on the ship was instantaneous. She had been leaping, now she seemed to lift from sea to sea, and tread down their crests into subjection.

'I think she'll stand a topmast stunsail,' Cruiser said to himself.

He went aft to watch the steering, which was grown the livelier for the sail. From the poop, he had a new impression of the power of her drive: she was swooping and swerving, like a thing alive; in fact she was a thing alive: she had ceased to be wood and iron, laden with cases: she was something of the spirit of the wind, and of the kindled wit of man, that laughed as she flew.

Suddenly, as he stood by the wheel, watching her head, and letting his eyes run aloft to the curves of the leeches under strain, the greyness in the heaven parted as though the sheets had given, with the effect of a sail suddenly let go and clewed up. The cloud tattered itself loose to windward and rived itself apart, and blue sky showed and spread. Instantly, a blueness and a brightness came upon the water. To leeward before them the storm passed away like a scroll. There, to port, far away, was the Chesil Beach, with the Needles beyond it, and the far and faint line of England stretching astern to the Start. The sun appeared and beauty came with him, so that all the tumbling and leaping brightness rejoiced.

One of the first things revealed was a fine clipper ship two miles ahead, lying almost the same course. On the starboard quarter, perhaps two miles away, another lofty ship came racing up Channel, and far astern a third showed. This third was perhaps not one of the China fleet.

'We've turned into the straight,' Cruiser said. 'There seem to be three left in it.'

'Yes, sir,' Fairford said, 'unless the race is already won.'

'We'll learn soon enough if it's already won,' Cruiser said. 'Get a tackle on the yardarm there,' he called. 'All hands set studding sails.' The mate and the men marvelled, but they leaped to the order. They were now as keen as Cruiser to bring their ship home. Not a man thought that perhaps the race had been already won by someone; to them the race was now beginning.

Cruiser was on the fo'c's'le head with the telescope trying to make out the ship ahead. Under the tapering cloud of sail he could see a dark green hull, with an old fashioned transom look about her stern. She could be no other than the *Caer Ocvran*. She had been running with prudence, not knowing where she was; now that the sky had cleared she was making sail.

'All ready, the foretopmast stunsail, sir,' Mr Fairford reported, adding under his breath, 'If you think she'll stand them, sir.'

'No time for prudence now,' Cruiser said, 'hoist away there – lively now.'

One at a time the mighty wings of studding sail swayed aloft and shook themselves out of their bundles with a roaring into service. Cruiser saw the topsail yard lift and the booms buckle as the strain came upon them; but the gear held. A whiteness boiled along the *Bird*'s side and flew in a sheet over the waist as she felt the new power given to her. Cruiser watched for a minute, standing well forward, eyeing the straining booms. 'They'll hold,' he thought, 'as long as the wind keeps steady and the helmsmen behave.' He crossed the fo'c's'le and eyed the ship ahead. She had set her lower studding sail, and no doubt was setting more as fast as the men could move, but the *Bird of Dawning* seemed sailing two feet to her one.

He watched for half a moment; Fairford and others were at his side, staring.

'Ah, she's holding us,' Fairford said suddenly. 'Yes, she's holding us. There go her topmast studding sails: beautifully done too. She's got forty hands at stations. It's something to have a full crew.'

'We've got twelve,' Cruiser said. 'Twelve good men upset the Roman Empire. Get the topgallant stunsails on her.'

The men ran to it: he slipped aft with the telescope, partly to con the ship, partly to see what the ship astern might be. He steadied the glass against a mizzen shroud and stared at the ship astern. She was on the starboard quarter, and plainly much nearer than she had been. She was not more than a mile and a half away. Not much of her showed except a tower of leaning sail, winged out with studding sails, a jib-boom poising and bowing, and a roll of white water under her bows. He broke off from his staring to rate Bauer at the lee wheel. 'Never mind what's astern of you,' he called. 'Watch your steering or you'll have the masts out of her and we'll skin you alive.'

He looked again at the ship astern. Someone forward had said that she was the *Min and Win*. He was satisfied that she was not the *Min and Win*, but a much bigger and newer ship, the *Fu-Kien*, commanded by a reckless dare-devil known as Bloody Bill China. 'Well, what Bill can carry we can drag,' he said, so he leaped down into the waist, to the job of getting more sail on to a ship that already had plenty.

'Doctor, there,' he called to Perrott, 'and you, Chedglow, get breakfast along on deck. Chedglow, get tongues and sardines and what you like out of the stores: the best there is. Hands must breakfast as they can, on deck, three at a time.' He watched the setting of the new sail and its effect upon the ship. She was holding her own now, perhaps gaining a very little on the *Caer Ocvran*, and hardly losing to the *Fu-Kien*.

'She's gaining on us, though,' Cruiser muttered. He could see how plainly, her anchors over the bows dripping brightness whenever she rose from the sea. 'Well, I'll try what the skysail will do. Up there, one of you, and loose the skysail.'

They loosed it and hoisted it, and had the sight of the pole bending like a whip of whalebone to the strain. Bill replied by loosing his main skysail, which blew away in the setting. They raced on now, hardly changing position. All hands in all three ships had all that they could do: getting a pull here, and pull there, a better set on this and a better trim to the other. Even Stratton, sullen as he was, seemed interested in the race; even Efans forgot his rights in the thought of how much better Captain Duntisbourne would have handled her. They raced in the laughing morning, while the coast slipped by them, all the landmarks long looked for. . . .

As he had expected, the change of the lifting of the gale brought with it a lessening of the wind and a shifting of it to two points to the northward. All three ships now had set every sail that they could carry, to the royal studding sails and trust-to-gods. Cruiser had guyed out a boom below the jibboom and had set a spritsail: Bloody Bill China had bonnets on his courses and contrivances that he called puffballs in the roaches of his topsails. What the *Caer Ocvran* was doing they could not clearly see: she was almost dead ahead of them. The three ships were drawing nearer to each other, the *Caer Ocvran* coming back, the *Fu-Kien* coming on. If the race had not been already won by some ship in ahead of them, it was the finest finish seen since the China prize was raced for.

An outward-bound ship came ratching past with the sprays like clouds of smoke at her bows. Her mate and various boys were on her fo'c's'le at work: they all knocked off to see those racers, no such sight had been seen in the Channel as those three driven clippers making the utmost of the day. Cruiser signalled to her an urgent signal, and asked, spelling the hoists, 'Has any China ship arrived yet?' He could see the ship's captain with a couple of boys busy at the signal halliards, acknowledging each hoist. The answer, when they made it, was the affirmative pennant without any ship's number to show the winning ship.

'So we're beaten to it, then, sir,' Fairford said. 'I wonder if the *Natuna* got it.'

Cruiser stared after the now receding ship, now being spoken by Bloody Bill, to whom she gave nothing but her own number, the *Inkerman* of London, and a dipped ensign.

'I don't believe she understood,' Cruiser said, 'and I'm not going to take that as gospel. We'll race these two ships at least.'

Still, something of the zest was gone from the contest when he thought that after all another ship might have docked even a couple of days before, and now lay discharging, with a gilt cock at her masthead. Then as the day drew on, the tide slackened and the wind dropped and shifted still more to the north: it gave them a beam sea and much anxiety for their gear, which held, but only just held.

At one that afternoon, as they passed Beachy all three ships began to feel the turn of the tide, the flying kites had to come in lest they should pitch the spars away. Then in little short spells of twenty minutes the wind would lull and the kites would be set again; and in this kind of sailing Bloody Bill China had an advantage: as Cruiser could see, he had the boys aloft in the tops all the time ready to race up to loose the light sail or take them in. He was creeping up a little and a little, and was now only about a mile astern, having gained certainly a mile and a half in five hours. In

another five hours the *Fu-Kien* would be half a mile ahead, having the pick of the tugs at the South Foreland. The *Caer Ocvran* was at a slight disadvantage, being not quite so happy in fresh or clearing weather as in light airs. However, her captain was fighting for every inch she lost. Cruiser with his small crew had only the miracle of the ship in his favour. He felt more and more keenly every instant that the ship was the best ship in the race. In other voyages she may not have been so: in this race all had conspired together, her builder and some happy combination in her trim, to make her supreme, but now she was short of hands, unable to do her best.

A darkness gathered into the heaven astern of them as the secondary moved up. The hours of the afternoon dragged by as the ships strained up Channel, all drawing nearer, all watched by thousands ashore, who now guessed that those moving beauties were the clippers of the China fleet.

Just off the Fairlight a little steamer, going with coals for Fowey, edged close in to the *Bird of Dawning*, so as to have a good look at her. Cruiser hailed her through the trumpet.

'Ahoy, there, the *Chaffinch*, what China ship won the Race?'

'No ship,' the *Chaffinch*'s skipper shouted back. 'You are the Race. Go in and win.'

'Thank you,' Cruiser shouted. 'Is that straight?'

'Yes. Get to it. Knock the bastards silly.'

This was greeted with a cheer from all hands: they had a chance still.

There came a sudden hurrying, greyness astern: it sent before it a hissing noise which put Cruiser's heart into his boots. He shouted out. 'Let go your royal halliards. Stand by topgallant braces,' and had let fly the main royal halliards as a rain squall swept over them and blotted out ships, sea and land in a deluge that filled the scupper. Out of the deluge there came wind in a gust that tore the flying royals into tatters. Something more than the royals went, the topgallant stunsails went at tack and halliards, blew out in the rain like dirty flags, flogged once, twice and away, with whips of their gear lashing around anything they touched. The masts bent, the yards curved at the arms under the pull of the sheets, and the ship leaped forward as though suddenly lashed.

The men ran to the gear: nothing more was lost: the split sails were cleared and new ones bent but not set. The rain made a darkness about them for twenty minutes, during which Cruiser had two men on the fo'c's'le looking out.

As the squall cleared off, the sun drawing to the west shone out and made a rainbow upon its darkness. Under the arch of colours they saw the *Caer Ocvran* not two hundred yards from them on the starboard bow. She seemed to be stuck there in tossing waters that whitened about her in a great bubble.

Through the glass Cruiser could plainly see her captain, pacing his weather poop, glancing quickly aloft and at the *Bird of Dawning*. 'Ah, yes, sir,' Fairford said, as he watched, 'you can glance and you can curse the helmsman, but the *Bird of Dawning*'s got you beat to the wide.'

'That's Captain Winstone,' Cruiser said. 'He was the mate of the *Bidassoa* when I was in her. Look at that now: did you ever see a ship so wet?'

'She's famous for it, sir; the *Caer*. A fine ship, too.'

Presently they were abreast of her, and forging ahead upon her, so that they could see her in her glory. She had a straight sheer and a transom stern, having been built upon the lines of the famous French frigate *L'Aigle*. In a light air no ship of her time could touch her, and she could run with the swiftest. She had a name through the seven seas for being wet: her decks now were running bright: for she was a caution in a head sea. They were watching and tending her now, getting some of her after-sail off her to keep her from burying her bow. Cruiser dipped his colours to her as he passed, but would not hail his old captain. As he drew clear, he saw her famous figurehead of Queen Gwenivere bowing down into the smother, then rising and pausing, then plunging down till the fo'c's'le rail was lipping green.

'Look at that,' Cruiser said. 'Did you ever see a ship pitch like that?'

As he spoke, she took a deeper 'scend than usual, and rose with a snapped stunsail boom lifting on a loose wing.

The *Fu-Kien* drew clear of the *Caer Ocvran* on her leeside: she was now a quarter of a mile away and gaining perhaps twenty yards a minute. Dungeness lay ahead, distant perhaps eight miles, and somewhere about Dungeness there would be pilots and perhaps tugs. There or thereabouts the race would be decided, another hour would see it out. Cruiser's men had been hard at it all day, and were showing signs of wear. They drank strong tea, syrupy with sugar and laced with brandy, as they got their hawsers ready forward and eyed the distant winning post.

All the issue from the gate of the Channel were about them: all the ships of a tide or two before from London and Antwerp, all the fishermen of Kent and Sussex. Every seaman who came past had no eyes for anything but those two superb clippers disputing for pride of place.

When the squall had passed by both had set every rag that could be brought to draw: they were now straining under clouds of canvas with a strong beam wind, and a head tide. Tarlton, who had been in the *Fu-Kien*, was not encouraging. 'Just the wind she likes most,' he said, 'she's a glutton for it. And she laps up a head sea like a rum milk-punch.' All the marvellous evening shone out mile after mile as they raced: the French coast plain as far as Calais, England white to windward, with occasional windows flashing like jewels, and a darkness of passing storm beyond. Occasional violent gusts kept men in both ships at the upper halliards; and still the *Fu-Kien* gained.

Cruiser was watching her now; she was not more than a hundred yards astern and to leeward, her decks full of men, and spare sails, all made up for bending, on each hatch, and the ship herself a picture of perfection, all bright for port, the paintwork and tarring finished; the hull black, with a white sheerstrake to set off her sheer, the yards black, man-of-war fashion, but with white yardarms, and her masts all scraped clean with glass, of shining yellow pine. All her brass was bright, and the scroll below her bowsprit had been freshly gilt. She was driving on easily with great laughing leaps. Cruiser could see, in the bearing of the men in her, their certainty that they were winning. Both ships were hauling their wind now to turn the bend. Both could see now, coming out from Dungeness, the pilot cutter, standing towards them, not two miles away, and beyond, making for them what seemed to be tugs, but might be small coasters.

'Too bad, sir,' old Fairford said. 'We'd have done it if we'd had a bit more luck.'

Cruiser was feeling broken-hearted at being passed on the post, but he could not take this view of it. 'No, no,' he said 'We've had such luck as no sailors ever had before. Think of what has come to us.' All the same, he had to move away. When he was on the lee-poop staring at the *Fu-Kien*, old Fairford could not see how bitterly he felt.

As they hauled their wind, the *Fu-Kien* forged ahead upon them, standing close in upon them, intending to weather upon them and drive across their bows. Bloody Bill China was there on his poop, an unmistakable big figure with a hard tall grey hat jammed sideways on his head and a long pistol in his right hand. 'That's Bloody Bill, sir,' Tarlton said to Mr Fairford. 'Bloody Bill China, sir, the Captain. You'll see him send a bottle of brandy out to the yardarm in a moment.'

Sure enough a lad with a line went up the mizzen-rigging and out to the crojack yard with it, rove it through a jewel block at the yardarm, and brought it down on deck. A bottle of brandy was hauled out to the yardarm upon it and dangled there. 'That's Bloody Bill's way, sir,' Tarlton said. 'If ever he weathers on a ship he shoots a bottle of brandy at the yardarm and then splits another on all hands.'

Twenty faces stared at the *Bird of Dawning* from the *Fu-Kien*'s side. Those men of the sea, negroes, Malays and Europeans, grinned and cheered as their ship slid past.

Bloody Bill China, who was certainly half drunk, shouted something to his steward, who was standing near the break of the poop beside a grog-kid. The steward put a corkscrew into the cork of a bottle which he held. Bloody Bill strode to the ship's rail, and yelled at Cruiser, whom he took to be Captain Miserden, 'Give my love to the Prophet Habakkuk.'

Voices from the *Fu-Kien*'s waist, eager for the promised grog and full of joy in their victory shouted 'Habakkuk, Yah Yah, Habakkuk,' and instantly the *Fu-Kien*'s mainmast was ahead of the *Bird of Dawning*'s mizzen, and at once the *Fu-Kien*'s crew manned the rail and cheered and beat the fire signal on both her bells. Bloody Bill China brandished his pistol above his head, brought it down, and fired it as he fell: the bottle at the yardarm was shattered – the brandy spilled. Instantly the steward drew his cork and Bloody Bill China shouted, 'Grog-oh! The *Fu-Kien* wins the China Race.'

She tore past the *Bird of Dawning*. She cleared her by a cable, then by three hundred yards. 'Look out, sir,' Tarlton cried to Cruiser. 'He'll cross your bows as sure as God made Sunday.'

And instantly Bloody Bill China did; he luffed up out of bravado, so as to get windward of the *Bird of Dawning*.

He was going to cross her bows, just to show her. As he luffed, one of the violent gusts beat down upon both ships. Cruiser saw it coming and let go in time, but it caught the *Fu-Kien* fairly, and whipped her topgallant masts clean off in succession as one might count one, two, three. The great weight of gear swung to and fro on each mast, the foreupper topsail went at the weather clew, the main-upper topsail halliards parted and the yard coming down brought the lower topsail with it, bending the truss and cockbilling the yard. The helmsman let her go off, she fell off, thumping and thrashing while gear came flying down from

the ruin. With a crash, the wreck of the foretopgallant mast, with its three yards, and stunsail booms and weight of sail and half a mile of rigging, collapsed about the forehatch.

It all had happened in a moment. Cruiser had been warned and had just time to heave the helm up. The *Bird of Dawning* always steered like a bird: she answered to a touch; she answered to it now, but the *Fu-Kien* was right athwart her hawse not three hundred yards away, falling off and coming down on her, with all the wreck on her mainmast visibly shaking the whole mast. One active daredevil soul was already racing with an axe to the splintered masthead, to hack through the shrouds.

Cruiser saw her come round almost on her heel, straight at the *Bird of Dawning*. For about half a minute it seemed certain that the two would go into each other and sink each other. The mizzen royal yard slid out of its bands and smote the *Fu-Kien*'s deck end-on like a harpoon. The terrified helmsman hove the helm hard down; the ship, having still way on her, swung back into the wind; with a running, ripping, walloping crash, her main topgallant wreck came down into her waist, going through the bunt of the mainsail as it went.

The *Bird of Dawning* went past her and missed her by thirty yards. As they passed, Bloody Bill China leaped on to the top of the wheelbox, hurled his hard hat at Cruiser, and while it was still in the air, settling to the sea, put three bullets through it with his pistol: he then hurled his pistol after it and leaped down cursing on to the main-deck to clear the wreck.

Cruiser left him to clear it; there, ranging down upon him, was the pilot cutter. In another minute that graceful boat rounded to with her pilot, who caught the tackle flung, and in an instant was swung high and brought upon the *Bird of Dawning*'s deck.

The Pilot was a short man of enormous breadth, with a gentle manner. He seemed puzzled at the smallness of the crew and at the unusual untidiness of the deck, the planks not scrubbed nor oiled, the paint not freshened. He came up the weather ladder to Cruiser and shook him by the hand.

'I'm proud to welcome you, Captain,' he said. 'You're the first China clipper to take a pilot this year.'

THE SAIL TRAINING ASSOCIATION

Racing and Sailing Rules including Seaworthiness, Safety Precautions and Equipment Regulations

*Any paragraph which is new or differs from the 1974 edition of these Rules and Regulations has an asterisk.

GENERAL

1. Composition of Crew

  (a) Sail Training Races are run for the benefit of young people and all vessels taking part must carry not less than their normal number of persons under training.

  *(b) For the purpose of these races, not less than 50% of the working complement must be persons under training (Trainees) between the following ages on the day on which the race or, in the case of a series of races, on the day on which the first race of the series, starts:

    (i) for major Sail Training Races (normally those in which Class A are eligible to take part) and for entries for the Boston Teapot Trophy – 16 and 25 inclusive (15 and 25 for Class A);

    (ii) for minor Sail Training Races (normally those in which Class B only may take part) and for entries for the Ince Trophy – 16 and 21 inclusive.

  The age limits for each race will be stated on the Entry Form.

  (c) Trainees are defined as follows:

    (i) young people who are being trained as future officers or ratings for entry into either the Naval or Mercantile Service.

    (ii) young people or others who are not training to become professional seamen, but who are being given experience in deep water sailing vessels as part of their schooling and/or character training. Trainees as defined above may be taken to be any young people within the age limits who are looking for a taste of adventure at sea, provided that they are not fully trained professional seamen and provided that they do not normally spend a great deal of their time sailing offshore as amateurs.

  (d) No person under the age of 16 (15 for Class A) is to be on board during a race, nor may any vessels with anyone under the age of 16 (15 for Class A) sail with a race (but not as a competitor) to take part in the associated events before and after the race.

  *(e) The above rules apply also to Cruises in Company except that trainees aged 15 may sail in Class B vessels only if they have temporarily joined them as part of a Crew Interchange organized by the S.T.A.

  (f) Any departure from these rules can only be approved by the Council of the Sail Training Association or by the Sailing Committee on their behalf.

2. Division between Classes

  (a) CLASS A. Square-riggers (ships, barques, etc.) of more than 150 tons Thames Measurement. Other vessels of 500 tons Thames Measurement and over may be included in Class A at the discretion of the Committee. There is no upper limit to the size of vessels in Class A.

  (b) CLASS B. All other sailing vessels with a low limit of size of 30 ft (9.14 m) in waterline length.

  (c) Entries in Class B may be subdivided into Divisions depending on the number of entries received, in accordance with their size and potential sailing ability.

    Note: In certain minor Sail Training Races, the low limit of size will be 24 ft (7.31 m) in waterline length. This will be made clear in race entry forms.

3. Observance of Rules

It is an essential part of offshore racing that the vessels sail at night, and at times out of sight of one another. An owner, or his representative, may therefore be the sole judge of whether the rules have been kept or not. He must, when signing his Declaration, be satisfied that no attempt has been made to win the race other than by fair sailing. A well-kept log is useful evidence in supporting or defending a protest.

*4. Multihulled Vessels
No multihulled vessel may take part in any Sail Training Race.

RACING RULES

10. General Authority of the Race Committee
All races, and vessels sailing therein, shall be under the direction of the Race Committee. All matters shall be subject to their approval and control; any questions and dispute which may arise shall be subject to their decision.

Their decision shall be based upon these rules so far as they apply, but, as no rules can be devised capable of meeting every incident and accident of sailing, the Race Committee shall have the power to make decisions in accordance with the customs of the sea. They will discourage all attempts to win a race by other means than fair sailing.

11. Rating
Each vessel must have a valid S.T.A. Rating Certificate before the start of a race. The Time Correction Factor (T.C.F.) of each competing vessel will be available together with Sailing Instructions, at the S.T.A. Race Office before the start of a race. The T.C.F. so listed at the start of the race shall be that from which the vessel's corrected time will be calculated, and shall be final for that race.

*Note: Rating Certificates dated prior to 1972 are now invalid. Rating Certificates dated 1972 to 1975 will apply in 1975 and new certificates will be issued for 1976.

12. Sailing Instructions
As far as possible the names and ratings of vessels competing in the race will be included in Sailing Instructions supplied to vessels, but these will not necessarily be complete or exact. Oral instructions shall not be given.

13. Start of the Race
A race starts from the starting signal, but a vessel shall be amenable to the S.T.A. Sailing Rules from the preparatory signal given five minutes before the starting signal of her Class or Division, until she either finishes the race or retires.

A vessel which has been entered and which manoeuvres in the vicinity of the starting line after the preparatory signal of her Class has been made shall be considered a starter whether or not she actually crosses the starting line.

A vessel starts when, after the starting signal, any part of her hull or equipment first crosses the starting line in the direction of the first mark.

14. Recalls
Recall numbers will not be displayed. If any part of a vessel, or vessels, be on or across the starting line when the signal to start is made, a gun will be fired, or suitable sound signal made, as soon as possible, and Numeral Pennant 0 (yellow and red) will be broken out. Any vessel over the starting line too soon shall return over the starting line or its extension and then cross the line in accordance with para. 13 above. If she fails to do so to the satisfaction of the Race Committee, the standard time penalty (see para 25(b)) shall be added to her elapsed time in the race unless she be disqualified by the Race Committee.

15. Vessels Arriving Late
Engines, or a tow, may be used ahead or astern up to the preparatory signal of the Class. If at the time of the preparatory signal a vessel is not within half a mile of the starting line, she may continue to use her engine or a tow until she is within half a mile of the starting line.

16. Finishing a Race
A vessel finishes when any part of her hull or equipment crosses the finishing line from the direction of the last mark, but continues amenable to the racing rules so long as any part of her hull or equipment remains on the line.

As soon as a vessel is clear of the finishing line she ceases to be amenable to the racing rules, except that she shall continue to observe any special regulations prescribed by the Sailing Instructions and shall keep clear of the finishing line and all other competitors who have not finished.

17. Navigation Lights and Fog Signals
Competing vessels must show port, starboard and stern lights from sunset to sunrise and must carry an adequate fog signalling apparatus.

All navigation and working lights must comply strictly with the provisions of the International Collision Regulations for the

Prevention of Collision at Sea.

The additional red over green lights on the mast are strongly recommended.

18. Joining, Leaving or Going Ashore During a Race

No restriction is placed upon persons joining the vessel, or leaving the vessel in order to take no further part in the race; but otherwise, crew, gear or stores may be taken to or from the shore only in the vessel's own boats propelled by oars.

19. Use of Engine

(a) An engine or power pump may not be used except for charging batteries, pumping bilges or supplying power for weighing anchor or hauling off except as in para 15 and para 19 (b), (d), (e) and (f). See also para 24 below.

(b) If an engine is used to recover a man overboard, to render assistance, or in any other grave emergency, full details must be reported in writing to the Race Committee as soon as possible after the completion of the race.

(c) If engines are used either ahead or astern between the preparatory and starting signals, the vessel shall have the standard time penalty (see para 25 (b)) added to her elapsed time in the race.

(d) Vessels of Class A may use their engines after the starting signal if it is necessary for the safety of the vessel to prevent her being driven ashore in the vicinity of the starting line. The length of time that engines have been used for this purpose must be declared on the Declaration Form at the end of the race, and this time, multiplied by one-tenth of her speed under power in smooth water, shall be added to her elapsed time in the race.

(e) If a vessel of Class A is recalled for crossing the starting line before the starting signal she may use her engines from the time of the starting signal until she recrosses the starting line in accordance with paras 13 and 14 above. No penalty will be imposed for this use of engines provided that the vessel does not thereby gain an advantage over vessels which do not cross the starting line before the starting signal.

(f) If, due to accident or illness, a member of the crew has to be put ashore, the engine may be used but a statement to this effect must accompany the Declaration. This statement must include all relevant information such as the time and position at which the engine was started to enable the Race Committee to decide what penalty, if any, should be added to the elapsed time. A time allowance will never be granted under this rule.

20. Means of Propulsion

No vessel shall employ any means of propulsion other than the natural action of the wind on the sails, nor may way be checked by abnormal means after the preparatory signal for her Class or Division except as in para 19 (d) and (e) above.

21. Steering

Automatic, mechanical and wind-vane devices for steering are prohibited.

22. Navigational Aids

All competitors may use any electronic or other navigational equipment normally carried on board.

23. Assistance from the Shore

(a) A vessel may **not** receive assistance from the shore by radio or other means which is not available to other competitors.

*(b) No vessel may take any stores or water on board during a race except in an emergency. If stores or water are taken on board during a race the circumstances must be reported on the Declaration Form at the end of the race.

24. Running Ashore or Fouling an Obstruction

A vessel after grounding or fouling a buoy, vessel or other obstruction, may use her own engines, anchors, boats, warps, spars and other gear to haul off, but shall not receive any assistance except from the crew of the vessel fouled. Any gear used shall be recovered before she finishes the race. If an engine is used for the purpose the circumstances must be reported to the Race Committee at the finish of the race.

25. Rule Infringements

(a) If a vessel receives assistance from persons not being members of her own crew (except as provided in para 24 above), or otherwise infringes or disobeys any of the Sailing and Racing Rules or Sailing Instructions prescribed by the S.T.A., she shall be penalised by having the standard time penalty (see para 25 (b)) added to her elapsed time or may be disqualified at the discretion of the Race Committee.

(b) The standard time penalty in hours will be one-tenth of the square root of the course distance plus 1.

Examples:

(i) For a course distance of 144 miles, the time penalty will be 2 hrs. 12 mins.

(ii) For a course distance of 2,500 miles, the time penalty will be 6 hrs.

26. Setting Sails

*(a) A vessel may set sails only in the position in which they are normally set and for which she has been measured and rated: i.e. vessels of Class A may not set special light weather or other headsails or between-mast staysails unless they are shown on the sail plans which have been supplied. The setting of stunsails and quadrilateral jibs is prohibited.

*(b) Headsails may not be boomed out on the windward side by a spinnaker boom or other device unless the entry form of the vessel concerned states that a spinnaker will be carried. This restriction on booming out headsails will **not apply** if all fore-and-aft sails set abaft a mast and with their luffs on a mast are stowed and provided that the area of the largest boomed out headsail is not greater than half the area of the mainsail (or areas of mainsail plus main topsail in the case of gaff rig).

27. Rounding Marks of the Course

A vessel shall sail the course in such a manner as to round or pass each **mark** on its required side and in correct sequence, and so that a string representing her wake from the time she starts until she finishes would, if drawn taut, lie on the required side of each mark.

When races are sailed in fog or at night, dead reckoning alone should not necessarily be accepted as evidence that a mark has been rounded or passed.

A vessel which in rounding or passing a mark, fouls it or causes the mark vessel to shift her position to avoid a foul, shall be disqualified or penalised unless on her protest it is established that she was wrongfully compelled to do so by another vessel.

28. Protests

A protest may be made by any competitor against another and the protesting vessel shall make every effort to inform the vessel protested against that a protest is being lodged.

All protests shall be in writing and shall state:

(a) The date, time and whereabouts of the incident.

(b) The particular rule, or rules, or sailing instructions alleged to have been broken or infringed.

(c) A description of the incident.

(d) Where required a diagram showing:

(i) the course, positions and tracks of the vessel/vessels concerned.

(ii) the direction and strength of wind and tide and depth of water if relevant.

The protest shall be signed by the owner or his representative and lodged with the Race Committee at the S.T.A. Race Office as soon as possible after the finish of the protesting vessel. It must be accompanied by a protest fee of £2 which will be returned unless the Race Committee consider the protest to be frivolous.

29. Declarations

A completed Declaration Form shall be lodged with the Race Committee at the S.T.A. Race Office as soon as practicable after the vessel has completed the race. Unnecessary delay in lodging the Declaration may result in the vessel being treated as having failed to complete the course.

Any contravention, however trivial, of any S.T.A. Sailing Rule, International Regulation for the Prevention of Collisions at Sea, or Safety Regulation must be reported. If a mark of the course is not sighted, this must be reported on the Declaration and must be accompanied by the log, or copy of the log and a track chart.

30. Time Limit for Sail Training Races

All Sail Training Races unless specified to the contrary in Sailing Instructions will have a time limit and the time of the end of each race will be published in the Sailing Instructions for the race.

*Elapsed times of vessels which have not crossed the finishing line by the time limit will be calculated from the formula:

$$\text{Elapsed Time} = T \times \left(\frac{D}{D\text{-}d} + \frac{0.2d}{D} \right)$$

D = the length of the course as published in Sailing Instructions

d = the distance of the vessel from the finishing line at the time limit

T = the time from the start of the race to the time limit

*31. **Timing**

The finishing time must be taken when the finishing line is crossed and this time must be recorded on the Declaration Form provided, immediately after the vessel has finished. The time should be taken accurately and the timekeeper should get another member of the crew to check this. This time must be certified on the Declaration Form by the Master and timekeeper. A time check should be obtained as close to the finish as possible.

*32. **Crew Lists**

No vessel may start in a Sail Training Race until her crew list, giving the name, an address (and telephone number if possible), and nationality of everyone on board in the race has been handed in at the Race Office. In the case of Trainees, their age at the start of the race, or in the case of a series of races on the day of the start of the first race, **and** their date of birth must be included. Failure to observe this rule will result in disqualification or such lesser penalty as the Race Committee may decide.

33. **Sail Numbers**

(a) All vessels of Class B must have a sail number. Any vessel which has not got a sail number will be issued with a number in the TS (Training Ship) series.

(b) If any vessel in Class B starts in a race without a sail number, she shall be penalised by having half the standard time penalty (see para 25 (b)) added to her elapsed time.

*34. **Class Flags and Ensigns**

Class A	First substitute of the International Code.
Class B Division I	Second substitute of the International code over numeral pennant 1.
Class B Division II	Second substitute of the International Code over numeral pennant 2.
Class B Division III	Second substitute of the International Code over numeral pennant 3.

All vessels **must** wear their appropriate ensign at the start and finish of a race.

*35. **Postponement Signals**

In the event of a postponement of a start being necessary, the following signals will be made from the vessel or shore station from which the starting signals are being made:

(a) 30-minute postponement: the answering pennant alone will be hoisted and two guns fired. This postponement may be repeated by firing two guns and dipping and re-hoisting the pennant.

(b) 6-hour postponement: the answering pennant will be hoisted over numeral pennant 6 and two guns will be fired.

(c) 24-hour postponement: the answering pennant will be hoisted over code flag A and three guns will be fired.

Note: The postponement signals given above will apply to all Classes which have not started at the time the signals are made.

SAILING RULES

*50. **General**

Sail Training Races will be started and sailed under the International Regulations for Preventing Collisions at Sea (I.Y.R.U. Rules do **not** apply at any time during S.T.A. races).

Owners are expected to ensure that persons in charge of vessels taking part in S.T.A. races are thoroughly familiar with all the current provisions of the Collision Regulations and understand their responsibilities with respect to these Regulations.

*51. **Fair Sailing**

A vessel shall only attempt to win a race by fair sailing and superior speed and skill. However, a vessel may be disqualified or penalized under this rule only in the case of a clear-cut violation of the above principle and not only if no other rule applies.

A proven breach of the Collision Regulations will be construed as **unfair** sailing and may result in disqualification or time penalty (see para 25 (b)).

*52. **Right of Way**

(a) If a right-of-way vessel is compelled to alter course to avoid collision with another vessel which ought to have kept clear, the former may protest.

Note : Attention is drawn to the following extract from the International Regulations for Preventing Collisions at Sea: 'In construing and complying with these Rules due regard shall be had to all dangers of navigation and collision and to any special circumstances, including the limitations of the vessels involved, which may make a departure from these Rules necessary to avoid immediate danger.' Please note the particular implications when related to situations involving fore-and-aft rigged vessels and square-rigged vessels, especially when proceeding to windward.

(b) Before the start, and until the starting line has been crossed, any vessel when making an alteration of course which may affect another vessel, must do so only at a speed and in a manner which will give reasonable opportunity to another vessel to avoid a collision.

(c) When passing marks of the course, the outside vessel shall give the inside vessel room to pass the mark on the correct side.

SEAWORTHINESS, SAFETY PRECAUTIONS AND EQUIPMENT REGULATIONS

*70. Seaworthiness

Every vessel taking part in a Sail Training Race or in a 'Cruise in Company' organized by the S.T.A. must be seaworthy and be equipped and sailed with proper caution. She must carry the essential equipment appropriate to the class listed in paras 71 and 72.

The S.T.A. will normally undertake inspection of some vessels after their entry has been received or before or after the race.

Any vessel taking part in a race shall be liable to disqualification or have the standard time penalty added to her elapsed time for not complying with these Regulations.

No complete list of specific requirements can be framed and compliance with the spirit of these Regulations is the sole responsibility of the racing owners whose attention is drawn to the certificates required of the owner on the Entry Form and Declaration.

Owners are reminded that they must anticipate spending long periods at sea where there may be no harbours or refuge within easy reach, and no means of obtaining assistance. Apart from assuring themselves of the soundness of the hull, caulking, standing and running gear, hard weather sails, etc., they should remember to look to such matters as rudder hangings, bobstay bolts, deck fittings, etc.; make sure that glass in deck openings, portholes, etc., can be protected easily and secured if broken; and that openings in the planking have seacocks on the flange of the opening, that propeller shafts are properly secured and cannot withdraw; that pumps are adequate and in good condition, can be worked at sea, and can be cleared easily in the event of choking.

71. Essential Equipment – Class A

All vessels of Class A must comply with the laws of their Country or the current Merchant Shipping Acts regulations regarding safety precautions and equipment.

72. Essential Equipment – Class B

All vessels of Class B must (unless permission has been authorized by the Sailing Committee) carry the following equipment which must be of a kind that is adequate and convenient for extended racing and cruising having regard to the size of the vessel.

(a) STORM CANVAS   Sail(s) capable of sailing to windward in heavy weather.

(b) LIFELINES   Strong and effective lifelines of wire rope or metal tube, or a combination of both, must be fitted right round the vessel, including the bow and stern, without a break. Lifelines must at no point be less than 24 in (61 cm) in height from deck level, and should be of adequate height in relation to the size of the vessel. If the distance between the rail cap and wire is greater than 18 in (46 cm), a second wire must be fitted approximately halfway between rail cap and upper wire; this second wire need not be carried further forward than the after upright of a pulpit at the bow. The lifelines must be supported at intervals of not more than 7 ft (2.13 m) and stanchion feet must be securely fastened to the hull. No lifelines need be fitted at points where bulwarks are 24 in (61 cm) or more in height. When a bowsprit is fitted, the lifelines need not be carried round the bow provided that there is a net below the bowsprit.

(c) LIFEBUOYS   At least two lifebuoys: they may be of circular shape or horseshoe shape and must be of adequate size and buoyancy. One of these, with a self-igniting buoy-light properly rigged, must be carried on deck within easy reach of the helmsman ready for instant use.

(d) LIFEJACKETS At least one inflatable or government approved type of lifejacket for each member of the crew must always be ready to hand. They should be tested regularly. It is also recommended that each lifejacket be equipped with a light.

(e) PERSONAL SAFETY HARNESS Must be provided for every member of the crew and should always be used in heavy weather by anyone on deck or in the cockpit. Only harness made specifically for the purpose is acceptable.

(f) LIFERAFTS Where Department of Trade and Industry or other Merchant Shipping Acts regulations or laws apply, these must be obeyed.

In all other cases, the following rules apply:

A liferaft (or liferafts) which is stable and capable of carrying the whole crew of the vessel with one compartment deflated, must be carried on deck (not under the dinghy) or in a special stowage opening immediately to the deck and containing the liferaft(s) only.

Every liferaft must comply with the following minimum requirements:

(i) It must be specially designed for, and solely for the use of, saving life at sea.

(ii) It must have at least two separate buoyancy compartments, each of which must be automatically inflatable.

(iii) It must have a canopy to cover the occupants and this must be automatically inflatable.

(iv) It must have in its pack at least:

1 sea anchor or drogue	1 bailer
1 bellows for hand inflation	1 repair kit
1 signalling torch	2 paddles
3 D.T.I. approved hand flares	1 safety knife
2 parachute flares	1 rescue quoit and line

(v) Each liferaft must have a valid annual certificate from the maker, or his approved servicing agent, certifying that it has been inspected, that it complies with the above requirements, and stating the number of persons that can be carried with one compartment deflated.

(g) DINGHIES A dinghy or boat of any type suitable for kedging and for use as the vessel's tender must be on board in addition to liferaft(s) but need not be carried on deck.

(h) DISTRESS SIGNALS To be stowed in waterproof container(s) and comprising at least the following.

> 4 red parachute flares
> 4 red hand flares
> 4 white hand flares
> 2 orange smoke day signals
> (Miniflares or pistol-fired flares may be used
> instead of hand flares)

(j) FOG SIGNAL An effective fog signal.

(k) BILGE PUMPS At least two adequate bilge pumps which can be operated independently at sea, one of which must be operable from the deck.

(l) FIRST AID Adequate first aid equipment with provision for dealing with burns.

(m) FIRE EXTINGUISHERS At least two chemical fire extinguishers in suitable and separate parts of the vessel, ready for instant use.

(n) ANCHORS AND CABLE Two anchors must be carried and suitable cables or warps, but if a warp is used for the main anchor, at least three fathoms of suitable chain must be fitted between the anchor and the warp.

(p) EMERGENCY STEERING GEAR Every vessel must be capable of being steered directly from the rudder stock. Vessels with wooden tillers must carry a spare tiller.

(q) RADAR REFLECTOR An effective radar reflector.

Note: Any vessel whose equipment meets with the requirements of the Royal Ocean Racing Club's Special Regulations Section B will be considered to meet the requirements of the Sail Training Association.

Competitors in the International Sail Training Races

Class A Square-riggers of more than 150 tons Thames measurement, and other vessels of 500 tons TM and over, at the discretion of the Committee.

Vessel	Country of registry	Rig	Thames tonnage	*T.C.F.	Complement	Race I	Race II	Race III	Race IV
Kruzenshtern	U.S.S.R.	4-masted barque	3,185	*.6499	236	X	X	X	
Libertad	Argentine	3-masted ship	2,587	*.6685	366			D**	
Esmeralda	Chile	4-masted barquentine	2,478	*.6658	327			X	
Juan Sebastian de Elcano	Spain	4-masted barquentine	2,478	*.6638	407		X	R	
Dar Pomorza	Poland	3-masted ship	1,784	*.6726	162	X	X	X	
Sagres II	Portugal	3-masted barque	1,784	*.6670	203		R	X	
Eagle	U.S.A.	3-masted barque	1,727	*.6857	212			X	
Gorch Fock II	W. Germany	3-masted barque	1,727	*.7451	173			X	
Mircea II	Rumania	3-masted barque	1,727	*.6991	187			X	
Tovarishch	U.S.S.R.	3-masted barque	1,505	*.6804	190	X	X	X	
Gloria	Colombia	3-masted barque	1,097	*.6662	145			X	
Danmark	Denmark	3-masted ship	845	*.6610	99			X	
Christian Radich	Norway	ship	773	*.6456	104	X	X	X	
Gazela Primeiro	U.S.A.	3-masted barquentine	445	*.6263				R	
Regina Maris	U.S.A.	3-masted barquentine	297	*.6085	45		R	X	
Erawan	Panama	barquentine	286	*.6553	16			R	
Unicorn	U.S.A.	brig	190	*.6550	22			X	
Phoenix	Eire	brigantine	151	*.6617	24	R	R	X	X

*Vessels in Class A raced without spinnakers and a 'no spinnaker allowance' has been included in the T.C.F.

D**: Disqualified after protest regarding collision at start at Bermuda

Figures for the ships' complements in Classes A and B are in some cases approximate.

R: Retired

Class B Division I Vessels racing without spinnakers

Vessel	Country of registry	Rig	Thames tonnage	*T.C.F.	Complement	Race I	Race II	Race III	Race IV
Te Vega	Panama	gaff schooner	380	*.7751	36			R	
Sir Winston Churchill	U.K.	3-masted topsail schooner	299	*.7794	55	X	X	X	
Artemis	Netherlands	3-masted topsail schooner	284	*.6028	12	X	R		
Gladan	Sweden	gaff schooner	232	*.7467	34	X	X	X	X
Eendracht	Netherlands	schooner	226	*.8311	37	X	R	X	
Sorrento	U.S.A.	bm. ketch	108	*.9072				R	
Astral	Netherlands Antilles	bm. ketch	195	*.9295	12			R	
Gefion	Cayman Is.	topsail schooner	189	*.6963	12	X	R	X	
Lindø	Cayman Is.	3-masted topsail schooner	176	*.6824	14	X	R	R	R
Westward	U.S.A.	staysail schooner	168	*.9216				R	
Zenobe Gramme	Belgium	bm. ketch	161	*.8029	15	X	R	X	X
Tabor Boy	U.S.A.	gaff schooner	127	*.7515				X	
Barba Negra	Canada	barquentine	123	*.6015	19			R	
Zew Morza	Poland	gaff schooner	118	*.7412	22	X	X	X	
Deliverance	U.S.A.	gaff schooner	116	*.7656				X	
Freelance	Antigua	schooner	108		20			R	
Camalot	U.S.A.	wishbone ketch	76	*.7735				X	

*Vessels in Class A and Class B Division I are racing without spinnakers and a 'no spinnaker allowance' has been included in the T.C.F. In accordance with S.T.A. regulations they are not permitted to use a spinnaker boom or other device to boom out a headsail on the windward side. In certain cases Class B vessels switched divisions for one or two races, and were given more lenient T.C.F.s when racing without spinnakers.

Vessel	Country of registry	Rig	Thames tonnage	*T.C.F.	Complement	Race I	Race II	Race III	Race IV
Ticonderoga	U.S.A.	bm. ketch	72	*.8532				X	
Escapade	U.S.A.	bm. yawl	70	*.8783				X	
Gedania	Poland	staysail schooner	63	*.9477				X	
Erika	Switzerland	gaff ketch	62	*.6957	8	X	R	R	R
Maruffa	U.S.A.	bm. yawl	55	*.7091	10			X	
Nis-Puk	W. Germany	gaff ketch	55	*.7242	4		R		
Valeda	U.K.	staysail schooner	55	*.8410				X	
Tina IV	W. Germany	bm. ketch	54	*.9255	7			R as Div II	X
Skookum III	U.S.A.	staysail schooner	54	*.8825	10			X	
William H. Albury	U.S.A.	gaff schooner	54	*.7488				X	
Wandering Star	U.K.	bm. ketch	53	*.8851		X			
Carola	W. Germany	gaff ketch	53	*.6658	11		X	X	X
Master Builder	U.K.	bm. ketch	50	*.9034	15	X	R	X	X
Yankee	U.S.A.	staysail schooner	49					R	
Black Pearl	U.S.A.	brigantine	41	*.6969				R	
Chief Aptakisic	U.S.A.	gaff schooner	38	*.7963				R	
Good Hope	U.S.A.	bm. sloop	38	*.8334				X	
Henri	Netherlands	gaff ketch	37	*.6612	8	R			
Blue Light	U.S.A.	bm. yawl	35	*.8721				X	
Windbourne	U.S.A.	bm. ketch	34	*.8466				R	
Gipsy Moth V	U.K.	staysail ketch	29	*.8690	7	X	X	X	X
Charm III	U.K.	staysail schooner	28	*.7989	8	R			
Voyager	U.S.A.	gaff schooner	22	*.6959				X	
Magic Venture	U.S.A.	bm. yawl	20	*.7695				R	
White Dolphin III	W. Germany	bm. sloop	14	*.8247				R	
Christine Marie	U.S.A.	gaff ketch	14	*.6500				X	
Candide	Panama	gaff schooner	14	*.7015				R	

Class B Division II Vessels racing with spinnakers

Vessel	Country of registry	Rig	Thames tonnage	T.C.F.	Complement	Race I	Race II	Race III	Race IV
Great Britain II	U.K.	bm. ketch	102	1.0550	21	X	X	X	X
Urania	Netherlands	bm. ketch	70	.8986	16	X	X	X	X
Stella Polare	Italy	bm. yawl	58	.9280	15		X	X	
Sayula II	Mexico	bm. ketch	57	.9801	9			X	
Germania VI	W. Germany	bm. yawl	56	.9604	17	X			X
The Empress	U.S.A.	bm. ketch	55	.9274	9			R	
Saracen	U.S.A.	bm. yawl	46	.9205	14		X	X as Div I	
Olinka	U.S.A.	bm. yawl	46	.9129				X	
Vega	Portugal	bm. sloop	45	.9046	12		X	X	
Dar Szczenia	Poland	bm. sloop	38	.9272	10	X	X	X	
Norseman	Netherlands	bm. ketch	38	.8889	16	X	R	R	X
Kukri	U.K.	bm. cutter	33	.9070	12	X	R	X	X
Sabre	U.K.	bm. yawl	33	.8998	12	X	X	X	X
Wojewoda Koszalinski	Poland	bm. ketch	33	.8718	10	X	X	X	
Walross III	W. Germany	bm. sloop	32	.9081	12	X	R	X	X as Div I
Hetman	Poland	bm. cutter	31	.8588	7	X	X	X	
Creidne	Eire	bm. ketch	30	.8969	12	X	R	R	
Caper	U.S.A.	bm. sloop	28	.8662	10			X	
Meteor	W. Germany	bm. sloop	27	.8401	6		X	X	
Stortebeker	W. Germany	bm. sloop	27	.8810	10	X	X	R	X
Carillion of Wight	U.K.	bm. sloop	24	.8469	10	X	X	X	X
Polonez	Poland	bm. ketch	22	.8575	6	X	X	X	
Outlaw	U.K.	bm. cutter	17	.8767	6	X	X	X	X
Tenerife	Spain	bm. sloop	18	.8237	7	X			
Active	U.S.A.	bm. yawl	14	.8270	10			X	
Dandy	U.S.A.	bm. yawl	14	.8270	10			X	
Fearless	U.S.A.	bm. yawl	14	.8270	10			X	
Flirt	U.S.A.	bm. yawl	14	.8270	10			X	
Glénan	France	bm. cutter	14	.8510	9	X	X	X	X
Cameo of Looe	U.K.	bm. cutter	14	.7921	6	X	X	X	X as Div I

Race Results

Race I – Plymouth to Santa Cruz de Tenerife

Class A	Elapsed time				Corrected time				Place	
Start 1200 B.S.T.	Days	Hr	Min	Sec	Days	Hr	Min	Sec	Division	Overall
Tovarishch	10	00	46	17	06	19	49	15	1	1
Kruzenshtern	10	15	33	00	06	22	04	55	2	2
Christian Radich	10	19	33	35	06	23	34	18	3	3
Dar Pomorza	10	10	10	29	07	00	16	03	4	4
Phoenix	Retired									

Class B Division I Start 1230 B.S.T.

	Days	Hr	Min	Sec	Days	Hr	Min	Sec	Division	Overall
Sir Winston Churchill	09	23	55	39	07	18	59	58	1	5
Gladan	10	12	30	18	07	20	32	44	2	6
Lindø	11	12	20	07	07	20	34	16	3	7
Zew Morza	10	19	21	15	08	00	14	00	4	8
Artemis	13	08	57	20	*08	01	28	19	5	9
Gefion	12	05	16	25	*08	12	12	23	6	12
Gipsy Moth V	09	22	23	16	08	15	09	32	7	13
Eendracht	10	13	58	08	08	19	04	24	8	15
Master Builder	10	06	58	44	09	07	07	14	9	21
Zenobe Gramme	11	19	57	30	09	11	59	24	10	24
Erika	13	17	33	35	*09	13	16	43	11	25
Wandering Star	12	01	17	44	10	16	03	20	12	30
Charm III, Henri	Retired									

Class B Division II Start 1245 B.S.T.

	Days	Hr	Min	Sec	Days	Hr	Min	Sec	Division	Overall
Tenerife	09	20	29	20	08	02	47	45	1	10
Glénan	*Disqualified				08	09	41	43	—	—
Kukri	09	07	02	08	08	10	17	35	2	11
Stortebeker	*Disqualified				08	14	11	26	—	—
Sabre	09	16	56	58	08	17	36	28	3	14
Carillion of Wight	10	13	38	20	08	22	48	24	4	16
Polonez	10	11	03	28	**08	23	16	53	5	17

Hetman	10	13	34	30	09	01	46	13	6	18
Dar Szczecina	09	19	54	33	09	02	44	06	7	19
Urania	10	04	19	35	09	03	33	06	8	20
Germania VI	*Disqualified				09	05	21	22	—	—
Walross III	*Disqualified				09	07	41	43	—	—
Outlaw	10	17	38	45	09	09	52	41	9	22
Great Britain II	08	23	12	17	09	11	02	27	10	23
Cameo of Looe	12	11	14	08	09	21	01	28	11	26
Norseman	11	06	09	40	10	00	08	46	12	27
Wojewoda Koszalinski	11	12	00	00	10	00	37	00	13	28
Creidne	11	15	26	02	10	11	00	56	14	29

**Includes Standard Time Penalty

Disqualified : These vessels were disqualified for infringement of Rule 1(b) of *Racing and Sailing Rules* (composition of crew). Their names have been included in the list in the position they would have taken had they not been disqualified.

Race II – Santa Cruz de Tenerife to Bermuda

Class A	**Elapsed time**				**Corrected time**				**Place**	
Start 1600 local time	**Days**	**Hr**	**Min**	**Sec**	**Days**	**Hr**	**Min**	**Sec**	**Division**	**Overall**
Tovarishch	Finished at sea				14	08	59	25	1	1
Kruzenshtern	At sea				15	21	21	11	2	2
Christian Radich	At sea				16	23	44	47	3	7
Dar Pomorza	At sea				17	20	22	46	4	11
Juan Sebastian de Elcano	At sea				19	07	12	33	5	18
Phoenix, Regina Maris, Sagres	Retired									

Class B Division I Start 1630 local time

Gipsy Moth V	18	23	30	20	16	11	50	03	1	5
Gladan	Finished at sea				16	12	49	29	2	6
Zew Morza	At sea				17	12	29	08	3	9
Sir Winston Churchill	At sea				18	03	27	18	4	13
Carola	At sea				23	16	05	42	5	25
Artemis, Eendracht, Erika, Gefion, Lindø, Master Builder, Zenobe Gramme	Retired									
Nis-Puk	Retired & *disqualified									

Class B Division II Start 1645 local time

Stella Polare	17	05	52	57	16	00	04	59	1	3
Stortebeker	*Disqualified				16	00	38	09	—	—
Great Britain II	15	13	54	26	16	10	28	19	2	4
Vega	19	07	18	49	17	09	18	15	3	8
Saracen	19	04	33	35	17	18	03	50	4	10
Sabre	20	06	26	24	18	02	50	03	5	12
Dar Szczecina	19	15	15	35	18	04	57	07	6	14
Carillion of Wight	Finished at sea				18	19	55	22	7	15
Urania	At sea				18	21	19	35	8	16
Outlaw	At sea				19	01	10	31	9	17
Polonez	At sea				19	14	42	57	10	19
Meteor	At sea				19	19	19	39	11	20
Hetman	At sea				19	20	36	04	12	21
Cameo of Looe	At sea				19	23	00	21	13	22
Glénan	At sea				20	03	15	41	14	23
Wojewoda Koszalinski	At sea				20	06	32	43	15	24
Creidne, Kukri, Norseman, Tina IV, Walross III	Retired									

*Disqualified : These vessels were disqualified for infringement of Rule 1(b) of Racing and Sailing Rules (composition of crew). Their names have been included in the list in the position they would have taken had they not been disqualified.

At sea : These vessels had not completed the course at the Time Limit for the race.

Race III – Bermuda to Newport, Rhode Island

Class A	Elapsed time				Corrected time				Place	
Start 1500 local time	Days	Hr	Min	Sec	Days	Hr	Min	Sec	Division	Overall
Gorch Fock	Finished at sea				06	07	00	43	1	—
Dar Pomorza	At sea				06	12	43	39	2	—
Christian Radich	At sea				06	19	52	06	3	—
Tovarishch	At sea				07	01	28	24	4	—
Danmark	At sea				07	04	18	09	5	—
Regina Maris	At sea				*07	06	50	09	6	—
Unicorn	At sea				07	10	37	09	7	—
Phoenix	At sea				07	10	59	05	8	—
Kruzenshtern	At sea				07	13	40	37	9	—
Gloria	At sea				*07	20	26	25	10	—
Sagres	At sea				*07	21	58	17	11	—
Mircea	At sea				07	22	34	03	12	—
Eagle	At sea				07	22	57	57	13	—
Esmeralda	At sea				09	08	36	21	14	—
Erawan, Gazela Primeiro, Juan Sebastian de Elcano	Retired									
Libertad	Disqualified as result of protest by *Juan Sebastian de Elcano*									

**Due to the prolonged calm early in this race the Time Limit for Class A vessels was brought forward by 54 hours to enable them to reach Newport at a reasonable time. For this reason Class A vessels are not included in the overall placings. The figures in this column refer to vessels in Class B Divisions I and II only.

*Includes Standard Time Penalty

Class B Division I Start 1530 local time

Ticonderoga	04	12	50	39	03	20	51	57	1	1
Escapade	04	14	26	25	04	00	59	59	2	3
Voyager	06	01	17	47	04	05	06	42	3	9
Saracen	04	21	51	40	04	06	32	21	4	12
Gladan	06	01	54	23	04	12	56	54	5	18
Camalot	05	22	28	27	04	14	12	14	6	19
Gefion	At sea				04	15	03	30	7	21
Good Hope	05	15	50	20	04	17	12	29	8	22
Carola	At sea				04	18	03	13	9	26
Gipsy Moth V	05	16	01	51	04	22	12	39	10	28
Veleda	05	23	08	21	05	00	22	48	11	31
Sir Winston Churchill	At sea				05	01	32	02	12	32
Maruffa	At sea				05	03	51	10	13	33
Zew Morza	At sea				05	04	17	15	14	34
Blue Light	05	23	11	09	05	04	52	21	15	35
Skookum III	06	00	06	39	05	07	10	40	16	36
Tabor Boy	At sea				05	07	52	06	17	37
Master Builder	05	21	40	46	05	07	59	35	18	38
Eendracht	At sea				05	12	44	20	19	39
Deliverance	At sea				05	14	05	31	20	40
Christine Marie	At sea				05	17	22	13	21	41
William H. Albury	At sea				05	21	15	43	22	42
Zenobe Gramme	At sea				06	08	29	51	23	44
Gedania	At sea				07	01	36	51	24	46

*Astral, Barba Negra, Black
   Pearl, Candide, Chief
   Aptakisic, Erika, Freelance,
   Lindø, Magic Venture,
   Sorrento, Te Vega,
   Westward, Windbourne,
   Yankee*   Retired

Class B Division II Start 1545 local time

Olinka	04	09	07	51	03	23	58	26	1	2
Hetman	04	17	06	53	04	01	08	34	2	4
Active	04	21	28	34	04	01	09	10	3	5
Dandy	04	21	42	45	04	01	20	53	4	6
Flirt	04	22	12	27	04	01	45	27	5	7
Fearless	05	01	34	51	04	04	32	50	6	8
Sayula II	04	08	02	15	04	05	58	01	7	10
Walross III	04	16	41	23	04	06	20	00	8	11
Stella Polare	04	14	55	42	04	06	56	29	9	13
Sabre	04	21	25	41	04	09	39	42	10	14
Urania	04	22	21	09	04	10	21	05	11	15
Kukri	04	21	44	53	04	10	47	57	12	16
Carillion of Wight	05	08	03	48	04	12	27	24	13	17
Vega	05	02	02	49	04	14	24	13	14	20
Polonez	05	12	22	10	04	17	30	24	15	23
Caper	05	11	08	12	04	17	35	26	16	24
Dar Szczecina	05	02	31	27	04	17	36	16	17	25
Outlaw	05	12	19	00	04	20	00	07	18	27
Meteor	05	21	34	07	04	22	58	27	19	29
Great Britain II	04	17	15	53	04	23	29	39	20	30
Glénan	Disqualified (Rule 1b)				05	00	49	14	—	—
Wojewoda Koszalinski	At sea				05	21	42	16	21	43
Cameo of Looe	At sea				06	12	46	39	22	45
Creidne, Norseman, Stortebeker, The Empress, Tina IV	Retired									

At sea : These vessels had not completed the course at the Time Limit.

Race IV – Boston to Plymouth

Class A

Start 1430 local time (with Class B Div. 1)	Elapsed time				Corrected time				Place	
	Days	Hr	Min	Sec	Days	Hr	Min	Sec	Division	Overall
Phoenix	34	06	35	55	22	16	18	48	1	13

Class B Division I Start 1430 local time

	Days	Hr	Min	Sec	Days	Hr	Min	Sec	Division	Overall
Gipsy Moth V	21	09	00	13	18	13	48	00	1	5
Gladan	24	22	37	11	18	14	59	21	2	6
Walross III	20	22	32	00	18	19	01	25	3	7
Carola	31	02	51	57	20	17	15	48	4	9
Master Builder	23	02	40	14	20	21	05	22	5	10
Tina IV	*Disqualified				21	06	43	30	—	—
Cameo of Looe	30	20	31	45	22	09	37	27	6	12
Zenobe Gramme	31	02	26	48	24	23	19	19	7	14
Erika, Lindø	Retired									

Class B Division II Start 1445 local time

	Days	Hr	Min	Sec	Days	Hr	Min	Sec	Division	Overall
Sabre	17	19	04	38	16	00	17	03	1	1
Kukri	18	09	28	33	16	16	25	07	2	2
Germania VI	*Disqualified				16	22	05	57	—	—
Glenan	*Disqualified				17	04	52	45	—	—
Carillion of Wight	21	03	16	00	17	21	36	15	3	3
Great Britain II	17	11	00	50	18	10	03	34	4	4
Stortebeker	*Disqualified				18	22	14	06	—	—
Outlaw	21	22	47	25	19	05	50	13	5	8
Urania	23	05	49	56	20	21	16	05	6	11
Norseman	Retired									

*Disqualified : These vessels were disqualified for infringement of Rule 1(b) of Racing and Sailing Rules (composition of crew). Their names have been included in the list in the position they would have taken had they not been disqualified.

THE SAIL TRAINING ASSOCIATION

International Sail Training Races 1976
Prize List

Plymouth to Santa Cruz de Tenerife Race

Overall Placings — **Prizes**

1st on Corrected Time
Tovarishch — His Majesty the King of Spain

2nd on Corrected Time
Kruzenshtern — Under Secretary of Merchant Marine for Spain

3rd on Corrected Time
Christian Radich — His Excellency the Minister of Commerce for Spain

Class A

1st on Corrected Time
Tovarishch — His Excellency the Minister of the Navy for Spain

2nd on Corrected Time
Kruzenshtern — His Excellency the Minister of Information and Tourism for Spain

3rd on Corrected Time
Christian Radich — Bernard Cayzer

4th on Corrected Time
Dar Pomorza — Bernard Cayzer

Class B Division I

1st on Corrected Time
Sir Winston Churchill — His Excellency the Minister of Foreign Affairs for Spain

2nd on Corrected Time
Gladan — His Excellency the Minister of Public Works for Spain

3rd on Corrected Time
Lindø — The Admiral Commanding the Maritime Zone of the Canaries

4th on Corrected Time
Zew Morza — The Mayor of Santa Cruz

5th on Corrected Time
Artemis — Bernard Cayzer

Class B Division II

1st on Corrected Time
Tenerife — His Excellency the Minister of State and Senior Vice-President for Home Affairs

Barbara Calder Challenge Cup for the winner of the class with the most entries
Tenerife

2nd on Corrected Time
Kukri — Chief of Staff of the Royal Spanish Navy

3rd on Corrected Time
Sabre — Civil Governor of the Province of Tenerife

4th on Corrected Time
Carillion of Wight — The Island Council of Tenerife

5th on Corrected Time
Polonez — Bernard Cayzer

6th on Corrected Time
Hetman — British Transport Docks Board

First to Finish
Great Britain II — His Excellency the Minister of Sport for Spain

Second to Finish
Kukri — The Captain General of the Canary Islands

Boston Teapot Trophy
Juan Sebastian de Elcano — For the greatest distance travelled in any period of 24 hours during 1974

Four additional prizes were presented by various local authorities in Tenerife to the yacht *Tenerife*.

Tenerife to Bermuda Race

Overall Placings

1st on Corrected Time
Tovarishch — H.R.H. The Duke of Edinburgh

2nd on Corrected Time
Kruzenshtern — Bermuda Chamber of Commerce

3rd on Corrected Time
Stella Polare — Bermuda Chamber of Commerce

Class A

1st on Corrected Time
Tovarishch — The Cape Horn Trophy

2nd on Corrected Time | The Pilgrims of Great Britain
Kruzenshtern
3rd on Corrected Time | Bermuda Chamber of Commerce
Christian Radich
4th on Corrected Time | Bermuda Government
Dar Pomorza
5th on Corrected Time | Bermuda Department of Tourism
Juan Sebastian de Elcano

Class B Division I
1st on Corrected Time | His Excellency the Governor of
Gipsy Moth V | Bermuda
2nd on Corrected Time | The Pilgrims of Great Britain
Gladan
3rd on Corrected Time | Bermuda Government
Zew Morza
4th on Corrected Time | Bermuda Government
Sir Winston Churchill
5th on Corrected Time | Bermuda Government
Erika

Class B Division II
1st on Corrected Time | The Mayor of Hamilton
Stella Polare
2nd on Corrected Time | Bermuda Chamber of Commerce
Great Britain II
3rd on Corrected Time | The Pilgrims of Great Britain
Vega
4th on Corrected Time | Bermuda Chamber of Commerce
Saracen
5th on Corrected Time | Bermuda Government
Dar Szczecina
6th on Corrected Time | Bermuda Government
Sabre

First to Finish
Great Britain II | Bermuda Department of Tourism
Second to Finish
Stella Polare | Bermuda Department of Tourism

Bermuda to Newport, Rhode Island Race

Class A
1st to Finish | Cutty Sark (U.S.A.)
Gorch Fock
1st on Corrected Time | Mr John Nicholas Brown Challenge
Gorch Fock | Trophy
2nd on Corrected Time | Allendale Insurance Co.
Dar Pomorza
3rd on Corrected Time | Booth High & Dry Gin
Christian Radich
4th on Corrected Time | Cayzer Irvine Company
Tovarishch

Class B Division I
1st to Finish | Rhode Island Marine Trade
Ticonderoga | Association
1st on Corrected Time | Rhode Island Marine Trade
Ticonderoga | Association
2nd on Corrected Time | Citizens Bank
Escapade
3rd on Corrected Time | Citizens Bank
Voyager
4th on Corrected Time | P. & O. Shipping Company
Saracen
5th on Corrected Time | Rowhotham & Son
Gladan
6th on Corrected Time | Southampton School of Navigation
Camalot

Class B Division II
1st to Finish | Aransons
Sayula II
1st on Corrected Time | Carter, Rice, Storrs & Bement
Olinka
2nd on Corrected Time | Mr & Mrs Edward W. Ricci
Hetman
3rd on Corrected Time | Horton, Church & Goff
Active

4th on Corrected Time
Dandy
Southampton School of Navigation

5th on Corrected Time
Flirt
British Army Sailing Association

6th on Corrected Time
Fearless
The London Sailing Project

Winner on Corrected Time in Class B Divisions I and II
Ticonderoga
Royal Globe Insurance Company

Overall Placings – Plymouth, England to Newport, R.I.

Overall Placings
1st on Corrected Time
Tovarishch
Textron, Inc.

Class A
1st on Corrected Time
Tovarishch
Outlet Company

2nd on Corrected Time
Christian Radich
Outlet Company

3rd on Corrected Time
Dar Pomorza
Outlet Company

Class B Division I
1st on Corrected Time
Gladan
Browne & Sharpe Manufacturing Co.
and S.T.A. Challenge Trophy –
The Florence Challenge Cup

2nd on Corrected Time
Sir Winston Churchill
Brown & Sharpe Manufacturing Co.

3rd on Corrected Time
Gipsy Moth V
Browne & Sharpe Manufacturing Co.

Class B Division II
1st on Corrected Time
Sabre
Amtrol, Inc. *and*
The Royal Thames Challenge Cup

2nd on Corrected Time
Carillion of Wight
C. O. Hoffacker Company

3rd on Corrected Time
Urania
C. O. Hoffacker Company

International Understanding
Zenobe Gramme
The Cutty Sark Trophy for International Understanding *and* The Hon. John Warner, Administrator of the American Revolution Bicentennial Administration

Retirement Award
Captain Jurkiewicz,
Dar Pormoza
Anonymous donor

Winning Square-rigger, Bermuda to Newport
The Captain, *Gorch Fock*
The Rolex Company

Winner – Best Elapsed Time, Plymouth to Newport
Great Britain II
Anonymous donor

Every Ship with Women Cadets
Rhode Island House of Representatives
A token certificate presented to a crew member from *Sir Winston Churchill* on behalf of the girl trainees.

Every Woman Cadet
Women of the Rhode Island Bicentennial Commission
A medallion presented to a crew member of *Astral* on behalf of the girl trainees (100 approximately).

First All-girl Crew to Finish, Bermuda to Newport
Sir Winston Churchill
Cutty Sark Scotch Whisky

A.S.T.A. Coastwise Race
First to Finish
Brilliant
Mr Perry Lewis *and* The City of Newport

Inshore Regatta
1st Place – Sailing
Vega
R.I. Bicentennial Commission

Class A – Tug of War   R.I. Bicentennial Commission
   Kruzenshtern
Class B – Tug of War   A. T. Cross Company
   Walross III
Swimming
   Class A: *Eagle*   R.I. Bicentennial Commission
   Class B Men: *Dandy*   R.I. Bicentennial Commission
   Class B Women:
   Sir Winston Churchill   A. T. Cross Company
Pulling Boats   R.I. Bicentennial Commission
   Dar Pomorza

Boston, Massachusetts to Plymouth, England Race

First to Finish
   Great Britain II   A cup presented by S.T.A.

Class A
   1st on Corrected Time   A tankard presented by S.T.A.
   Phoenix

Class B Division I
   1st on Corrected Time   A tankard presented by S.T.A.
   Gipsy Moth V

Class B Division II
   1st on Corrected Time   A tankard presented by S.T.A.
   Sabre

Index